home
Inspirations

home Inspirations

Over 60 decorative projects for every room in the home

DEBORAH BARKER

LORENZ BOOKS

First published by Lorenz Books in 1999

This edition distributed in Canada by Raincoast Books,
8680 Cambie Street
Vancouver, British Columbia V6P 6MP

© Anness Publishing Limited 1999

Lorenz Books is an imprint of
Anness Publishing Limited
Hermes House
88–89 Blackfriars Road
London SE1 8HA

A CIP catalogue copy of this book is available from the British Library

Publisher	Joanna Lorenz
Project Editors	Jeremy Smith, Emma Hardy
Designer	Ian Sandom
Production Controller	Steve Lang
Photographers	Rodney Forte, Tim Imrie, Rose Jones, Lizzie Orme, Stephen Pam, David Parmiter, Graham Rae, Adrian Taylor, Lucy Tizard, Debi Treloar
Project Contributors	Helen Baird, Lisa Brown, Victoria Brown, Sacha Cohen, Marion Elliot, Mary Fellows, Alison Jenkins, Deirdre O'Malley, Maggie Philo, Isabel Stanley, Josephine Whitfield
Illustrators	Madeleine David and Lucinda Ganderton
Stylists	Lisa Brown, Katie Gibbs, Labeena Ishaque, Leann Mackensie, Jo Rigg, Fanny Ward, Judy Williams

Printed and bound in Singapore

10 9 8 7 6 5 4 3 2 1

Contents

Introduction

In the past, home decorating meant little more than searching forlornly for materials that were featured in expensive magazines. You would find yourself settling for a coat of gloss on the walls and re-carpeting the house at great expense before the checking the terrible damage wrought upon your bank balance.

Today, however, there can be no such excuses. Modern fabrics and equipment open up a range of possibilities to the creative home decorator that needn't cost huge sums of money and require nothing more than a little thought and imagination.

Working its way around the house, *Home Inspirations* features an exciting selection of projects, from complete room treatments to beautiful accessories. Using innovative and contemporary techniques, such as stamping and stencilling, and a plethora of paint effects and craft skills, the book is intended to encourage you to cast aside timidity and opt for bold, adventurous alterations.

It shows you how to create an extravagant Santa Fe style wall decoration for a living room, a grandiose gothic design for a dining room, a lavish Tuscan decoration that will revolutionize your study and introduce a riot of colour into your bedroom with an unabashed pink wall. These inspirational projects reveal how, by side-stepping traditional materials, you can make truly original changes. Why not introduce the Atlantic into your bathroom by adding a dramatic mosaic floor with a seafaring motif? For treating natural light sources, why not use woven organza to

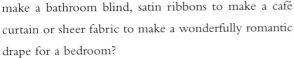

make a bathroom blind, satin ribbons to make a café curtain or sheer fabric to make a wonderfully romantic drape for a bedroom?

Inspired decorators will find it easy to work miracles around the home by simply using what they already have, rather than purchasing costly new items. Neglected rooms and accessories can often be rescued by the simplest of alterations. Dry brush an ordinary kitchen chair, for example, to create a Scandinavian-style antique centrepiece or add a decoupage wall plaque to a hallway door to create a striking entrance. Alternatively, thread a dowdy blanket with beads to create an eye-catching throw for a favourite chair or decorate a lamp base with mosaics to create a genuine focal point.

Beautiful accessories enable you to express your creativity and to let your imagination run riot – they can be used to imbue a room with your personality, using a selection of easy craft skills. Make a stained glass

sunlight catcher to lighten a dusty study or a papier-mâché nautical wall store (cabinet), a beaded splashback or a hand-painted china bath set to emphasize the watery origins of your bathroom. Hand-painted china mugs in a kitchen are sure to be noticed while highly decorated salt and pepper shakers in the dining room provide a finishing touch to any meal or get-together.

The projects in this book range from the simple to the more complicated, so there is something for every level of expertise and ability. Each project is carefully explained and comes complete with step-by-step instructions and photographs. A techniques section at the back of the book takes you through the more difficult sewing skills and provides tips on craft skills such as grouting and making papier-mâché.

Armed with such an array of inspirational ideas to revamp and revolutionize your home, you will soon find that decorating can be great fun and that the only limits are your imagination!

living rooms

The living room is the ideal place to relax, away from the stresses of the world, and to enjoy good conversation and the company of others – so it deserves to be decorated with care.

The walls are perhaps the first feature you notice when you walk into a room and, with the world getting ever smaller, why not draw on worldwide influences when you are decorating? Transform your living room with a Santa Fe style motif or add a touch of continental elegance with a frieze frame border.

Windows are critical to the ambience of a room, and the way you treat them can make a real difference. To evoke a little Mediterranean chic, hang striped voile curtains or introduce a stamped calico blind to gently diffuse the light.

Artificial light sources deserve a makeover too, so swathe an ordinary lampshade in purple silk to make a real focal point or dress up an uninspiring lamp base with beautiful mosaics to create a sophisticated centrepiece.

Finally, in a room where people will spend time relaxing, ensure that the seating is appealing. Festoon a dowdy throw with shimmering beads, turn a plain cushion into a silk sensation or transform a chair with a beaded cover to really catch the eye.

Transforming your living room doesn't mean having to commit yourself to sweeping changes or spiralling debt. All it requires is using what you already have and concentrating on the details. The only thing the home decorator really needs is a dash of ingenuity.

SANTA FE STRIPES

Aztec motifs, like this bird, are bold, stylized and one-dimensional, and translate perfectly into stamps. Strong colour contrasts suit this style, but here the pattern is confined to widely spaced stripes over a cool white wall, and further restrained with a final light wash of white paint.

YOU WILL NEED

matt emulsion (latex) paints in off-white, warm white, deep red
and navy blue
paint-mixing container
natural sponge
broad and medium paintbrushes
plumbline
ruler
pencil
masking tape
marker pen
medium-density sponge, such as a household sponge
craft knife and cutting mat
small paint roller
old plate
high-density sponge, such as upholstery foam (foam rubber)

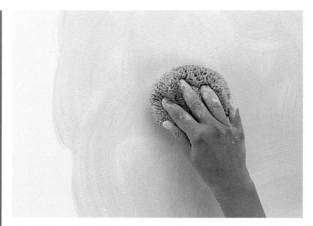

1 Dilute the off-white emulsion (latex) with 50% water and apply a wash over the wall using a sponge, alternating the angle at which you work. Allow to dry.

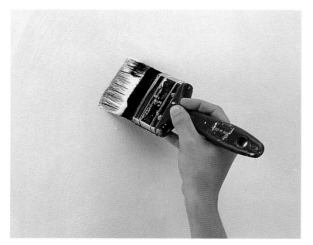

2 Using a broad, dry brush, apply warm white emulsion in some areas of the wall to achieve a rough-looking surface. Allow to dry.

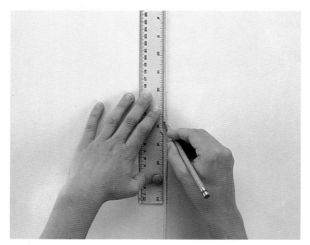

3 Starting 10cm/4in from one corner, and using a plumbline as a guide, draw a straight line from the top to the bottom of the wall.

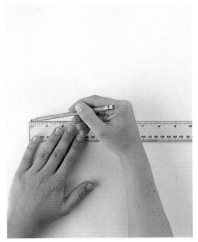

4 Measure 45cm/18in along the wall, hang the plumbline again and mark a second vertical line. Draw another line 10cm/4in away to create a band. Repeat all across the wall.

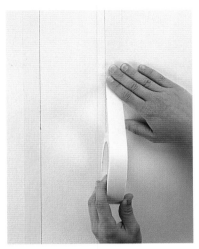

5 Apply masking tape to the wall on each outer edge of the marked bands.

6 Paint the bands in deep red emulsion. Leave to dry.

7 Draw a 10 x 20cm/4 x 8in diamond shape on a medium-density sponge and cut out the shape using a craft knife and cutting mat.

8 Use a small roller to load the stamp with navy blue emulsion paint and stamp the diamonds down the red bands, starting from the top and just touching at their tips.

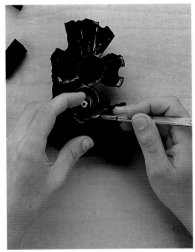

9 Copy the bird template at the back of the book on to a piece of high-density sponge. Cut away the excess sponge using a craft knife.

10 Use the roller to load the bird stamp with off-white emulsion (latex) and print the birds upright, roughly in the centre of the diamonds.

11 When the motifs are dry, use minimal pressure and a dry brush to brush gently over each band with warm white emulsion.

FRIEZE FRAME

If you can't find a wallpaper border that you like, then why not make your own? Just measure the walls of the room and copy as many motifs as you need to fit. Paint the border to match the colour of your room for a truly individual look.

YOU WILL NEED
lining paper
ruler
craft knife
yellow emulsion (latex) paint
medium paintbrushes
PVA (white) glue
small, sharp scissors
green paper
yellow ochre acrylic paint

1 Measure the lining paper to the required length and depth of your frieze. Cut along the edge using a ruler and craft knife.

2 Mix three parts yellow emulsion (latex) paint with one part glue. Add a little water to allow the mixture to flow more easily. Use this to paint the lining paper.

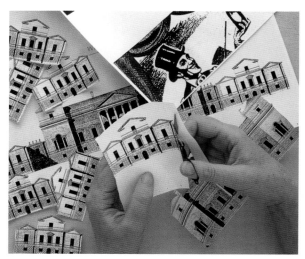

3 Photocopy the frieze motifs at the back of the book enough times to cover the length of the border. Cut them out with scissors.

4 Cut the green paper into equal short lengths. Tear along the top edge to represent greenery.

5 Arrange and glue down the buildings and torn paper along the length of the frieze.

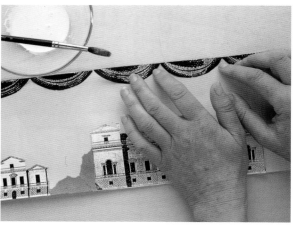

6 Glue down the swag motifs along the top edge of the frieze.

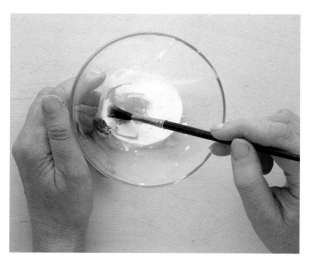

7 Mix a little yellow ochre acrylic paint into some PVA (white) glue. Then dilute four parts tinted glue with one part water.

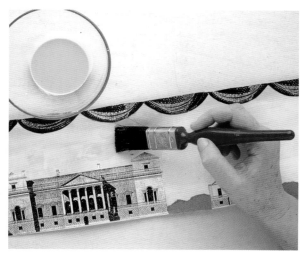

8 Brush the tinted, diluted glue over the frieze to seal and protect it.

VOILE STRIPED CURTAINS

Sheer, unstructured curtains in a mixture of brilliant colours have an ethnic feel.
Choose a colour for the backing panel that will enhance the mixture and increase its richness.
You can sew the sides or leave them hanging free as shown overleaf.

YOU WILL NEED
tape measure
scissors
voile fabrics in three colours
tailor's chalk
pins
sewing machine
matching threads
iron
voile backing fabric
2.5cm/1in wide ribbon or braid
9mm/³/₈in satin ribbon

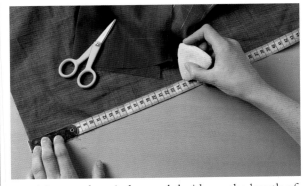

1 Measure the window and decide on the length of the curtains. Cut the voile fabrics into six panels (three per curtain) that will make a total width at least one and a half times that of the window. In each curtain shown overleaf, the two outside panels are the same width and the centre panel is slightly wider. Add 3cm/1¼in to the length for the seam allowances.

2 With right sides together, pin each centre panel to one of the side panels and machine-stitch with a 1cm/½in seam allowance. Sew on the other side panels. Press the seams open. Cut the backing fabric to the same size as the curtains.

3 Cut a length of 2.5cm/1in ribbon or braid for each joined seam and pin it over the seam. Machine-stitch in place down both edges.

▶

4 Fold over, press and machine-stitch a double 1cm/½in hem down each side of the curtains and along the lower edge. Repeat around the sides and lower edge of the backing fabric.

5 Cut some lengths of 9mm/⅜in satin ribbon, long enough to fit over the curtain pole, for the hanging loops. Fold the loops in half and pin the raw edges to the top edge of the curtains, spacing them evenly about 20cm/8in apart.

6 Pin the backing fabric to each curtain along the top edge, right sides together, and machine-stitch, trapping the ribbon loops. Turn the backing fabric to the back of the curtain and press the seam.

18

STAMPED CALICO BLIND

Ready-made stamps are available in hundreds of different shapes: use them with fabric paints to create made-to-measure designs for curtains and blinds. Here, the cords are threaded through large eyelets that are decorative as well as functional.

YOU WILL NEED
tape measure
scissors
medium-weight calico
pins
fabric paints
plate
applicator sponges
high-density foam stamps
iron

sewing machine
matching thread
needle
pencil
eyelet kit
1.5cm/⅝in brass eyelets
nylon cord
2 spring toggles
9mm/⅜in wooden dowel
2 screw-in hooks

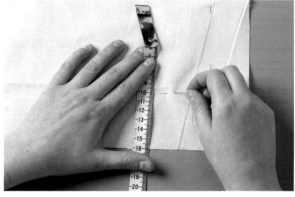

1 Measure the window to establish the finished size of the blind. Cut two pieces of calico to these measurements, adding 4cm/1½in to the width and 7cm/2¾in to the length. On one piece, use pins to mark out the area for the stamped design, allowing 5cm/2in on either side for the eyelets, 3cm/1¼in at the top and 6cm/2½in at the bottom.

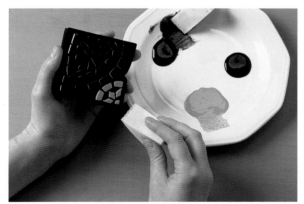

2 Squeeze out a small amount of each fabric paint on to a plate. Using an applicator sponge, apply an even coating of paint to the first stamp.

3 Stamp your design on to the calico, applying an even pressure. Apply fresh paint to the stamp for each motif to keep the colour consistent.

4 Complete the design and leave to dry. Iron the calico on the wrong side to fix (set) the paint.

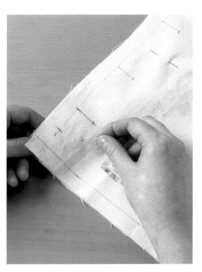

5 With right sides together, pin the printed calico to the plain piece of calico around all the edges.

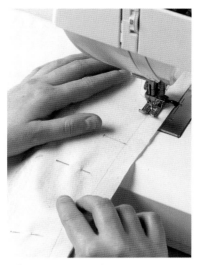

6 With a 2cm/¾in seam allowance at the top and sides and a 5cm/2in allowance at the bottom, machine-stitch the edges, leaving a 15cm/6in gap on one side and a 2cm/¾in gap at the top of each side seam.

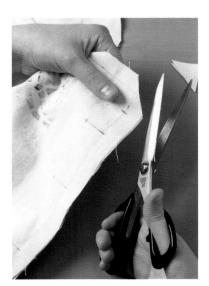

7 Clip the seam allowance at the corners.

8 Turn the blind right side out through the gap left in the side seam.

9 Press flat all the edges of the blind.

▶

10 Slip-stitch the gap in the side seam by hand to close.

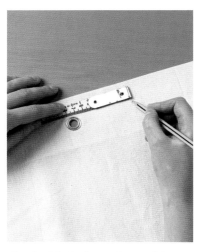

11 Mark the eyelet positions up each side of the blind about 7.5cm/3in apart. Insert the eyelets using a kit.

12 Thread a length of nylon cord through the eyelets on each side of the blind, knotting it at the top.

13 Thread the bottom end of each length of cord through a spring toggle.

14 Finish the cord at the bottom with a knot and trim off the excess.

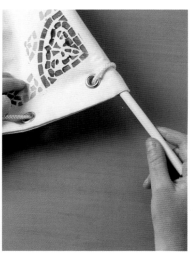

15 Cut a length of dowel 4cm/1½in wider than the blind and thread it through the gaps in the top corners. Screw two hooks into the top corners of the window frame from which to hang the blind.

BEADED THROW

Brightly painted wooden beads are ideal for fringing a plain cotton throw, as they are light in weight and tend to have large holes. Combine them with the occasional metallic bead to catch the light and give definition to the design.

YOU WILL NEED
florist's wire
wire cutters
ready-made throw with fringe
small, medium and large wooden beads in
various colours
brass beads

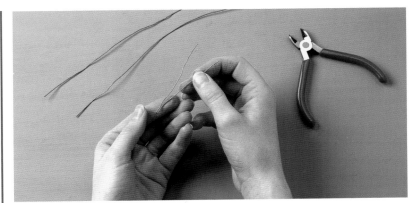

1 Make a threading device by cutting a short length of florist's wire and bending it in two.

2 Decide on the design for your fringe. This throw had 60 lengths of fringe, each knotted at the top. Every other length was beaded with one medium, one small and one large wooden bead and two brass beads, alternating the colours of the large beads. It took 30 small and medium beads, 15 of each of the coloured large beads and 60 brass beads to fringe one end of the throw. Untie the top knot of each length of fringe that is to be beaded. Thread on a brass bead using the wire threader.

3 Twist the fringe to secure stray ends and tie a knot to sit close to the brass bead.

4 Thread on a small bead, then a large bead, a medium bead and finally a second brass bead. Tie a knot as before.

5 There are many variations for decorating a fringe with beads. For example, you could plait (braid) the fringe and add a coloured bead followed by a brass bead.

6 Another idea is to join two lengths of fringe together with one bead. Thread contrasting smaller beads followed by a brass bead to each length of fringe and knot the ends.

SILK TRELLIS CUSHION

The unusual fringing made from the main silk fabric is easy to sew, and yet looks really effective. Choose toning (complementary) buttons to hold the trelliswork in place and for fastening the rouleau loops on the back. Finish with a tassel at each corner, made from the same silk dupion.

YOU WILL NEED
55cm/22in of 115cm-/45in-wide grey silk dupion
sewing thread
23 shell buttons
blunt needle or safety pin
four 15mm/⅝in cotton balls
55 x 30cm/22 x 12in cushion pad

1 For the cushion front, cut a piece of grey silk 58 x 33cm/23 x 13in. For the trelliswork, cut several strips of silk 2.5cm/1½in wide. On each strip fold one long edge over by 1cm/½in, and top-stitch 2mm/¹⁄₁₆in from the folded edge. Using a needle, carefully separate and remove the threads from both raw edges, pulling away the threads right up to the seamline to make a fringe.

2 Arrange the frayed strips on the cushion front in a lattice pattern, with the parallel strips placed 11cm/4¼in apart.

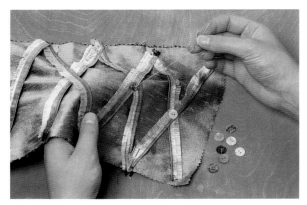

3 Sew a button at each of the intersections, then stitch all around the edge of the fabric to hold the strips in position. ▶

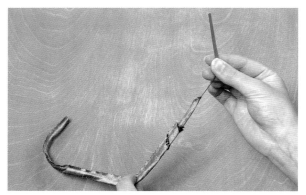

4 To make the rouleau loops, cut a strip of fabric 33 x 3 cm/13 x 1¼ in. Fold in half lengthways with right sides together, and machine stitch 6 mm/ ¼ in from the folded edge. Attach a thread to one end and pass the strip through the eye of a blunt needle or a safety pin, then push the needle or safety pin through the tube to turn the loop right side out. Cut the strip into three 11 cm/4½ in lengths. For the cushion back, cut one piece of fabric 20 x 33 cm/ 8 x 13 in and one piece 51 x 33 cm/20¼ x 13 in.

5 On the smaller back piece, turn and press a 2 cm-/¾ in-wide double hem on one long edge. On one short edge of the larger piece, position and pin the three rouleau loops, checking that the loops will fit over the buttons. Tack (baste) and machine stitch the loops in place. Cut a facing 33 x 5 cm/13 x 2 in, and neaten one long edge. With right sides together, pin and machine stitch the facing over the rouleau loops. Turn and press the facing to the wrong side and then top stitch.

6 For each tassel, cut two pieces of fabric 10 cm/ 4 in square. Work zigzag stitch 1.5 cm/⅝ in from the raw edges. Fray the edges (see Step 1), pulling away threads up to the stitched line.

7 Mark a 5 cm-/2 in-diameter circle in the centre of the square. Run a gathering thread along the marked line. Place a cotton ball in the centre, draw up the gathers and secure them, then wind the thread around the gathering thread and secure with a stitch. Insert the needle inside the cotton ball and bring it out at the top of the tassel, then stitch to one corner of the cushion. Repeat to make three more tassels. Insert the cushion pad and fasten the rouleau loops.

BEADED CHAIR COVER

Beads add texture and detail to this child-like, stylized flower decoration for a loose chair cover. In a design of strong shapes and colour contrasts, created in sturdy fabrics, their delicacy creates a delightful surprise.

YOU WILL NEED
iron
fusible bonding web
scraps of cotton fabrics in three colours
card (card stock) for template
pencil
scissors
sewing machine
matching sewing threads
beading needle
small glass rocaille beads
bugle beads
assorted round glass beads
canvas chair cover
dressmaker's pins
needle and tacking (basting) thread

1 Iron fusible bonding web to the wrong side of the fabrics you have chosen for the flower appliqué.

2 Copy the templates at the back of the book for the petal and flower centre. Draw around the petal template on the backing paper and cut out 12 shapes. Cut out the circular centre for the flower from a contrasting fabric.

3 Arrange the petals on a square of the background fabric, peel off the backing paper and iron them in place. Iron on the flower centre.

▶

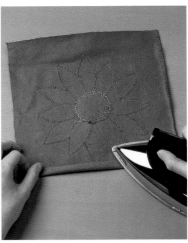

4 Stitch around the shapes using a decorative stitch such as zig-zag stitch or satin stitch.

5 Decorate the flower centre and petals with an assortment of evenly spaced glass rocaille and bugle beads.

6 Fold in the raw edges of the background square and press in place.

7 Following the folded seam line, sew on an assortment of small and medium-sized round glass beads in various assorted colours, stitching them about 1 cm/½ in apart.

8 Position the appliqué panel on the back of the chair cover. Pin and tack (baste) it in place, then machine-stitch it close to the edge.

MOSAIC LAMP BASE

A breeze (concrete) block makes a safe, solid base for a large floor lamp. Cover it in a chunky floral design made of floor tiles, marble and tiny pieces of mirror, set into the gaps to catch the light from the lamp.

YOU WILL NEED
breeze (concrete) block
ruler
soft pencil
drill, with a long bit (at least half the length of the block)
chisel
lamp flex (cord)
hollow metal rod, with a thread cut into it
rubber (latex) gloves
cement-based tile adhesive
piece of chalk
protective goggles
rubber (latex) gloves
ceramic floor tiles, in yellow and one other colour
piece of sacking (heavy cloth)
hammer
flexible (putty) knife
white marble tiles
tile nippers
mirror glass
notched spreader
sponge
dust mask
sandpaper
lamp fittings
short piece of copper pipe
plug
screwdriver
soft cloth

1 On one end of the breeze (concrete) block, mark diagonal lines to find the centre. Drill a hole right through the centre, turning the block over if necessary to drill from the other end.

2 On one end, use a chisel to cut a deep groove to contain the flex (cord), from the centre hole to one edge. This will be the bottom of the lamp base.

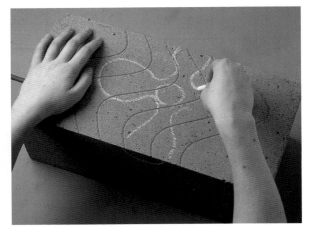

3 Thread the flex (cord) through the centre hole, leaving a long length at the bottom. At the top, pass it through the metal rod as shown. Lay the block on its side and pull the flex through the groove. Wearing rubber (latex) gloves, mix some tile adhesive according to the manufacturer's instructions, and fill in the groove to secure the flex. Leave to dry.

4 Using a piece of chalk, draw a large, simple flower design on the sides of the breeze (concrete) block, either free-hand or tracing the template from the back of the book. Exclude the bottom of the block. Plan out the colour scheme for your petals, keeping the yellow for the flower centres and white for the background.

5 Wearing goggles and rubber (latex) gloves, wrap each floor tile in sacking (heavy cloth) and break it up into pieces with a hammer. Using a flexible (putty) knife and wearing rubber gloves, spread tile adhesive over each flower shape. Press the yellow tesserae (tiles) into the adhesive and build up the flower centres. Continue with the petals until they are all covered.

6 Wearing goggles and heavy gloves, wrap each white marble tile in sacking (heavy cloth) and break it into pieces with the hammer. Working on a small area at a time, wearing rubber gloves, spread tile adhesive over the background and press in the marble pieces. Don't worry if your pieces don't butt up to each other. Leave to dry overnight.

7 Using tile nippers and wearing goggles, cut the mirror glass into small fragments. Wearing rubber gloves, insert blobs of tile adhesive in the larger gaps between the tesserae. Wearing heavy gloves, push in the mirror fragments, checking that they are level with the rest. Continue inserting mirrored pieces over the base until covered. Leave to dry overnight.

8 Wearing rubber gloves, grout the lamp base by scraping tile adhesive over the surface with a notched spreader. This will bind all the pieces of tesserae together firmly. Use your gloved fingers to smooth it right into the fissures, and along the sides of the block. Wipe off the excess tile adhesive with a damp sponge and leave to dry overnight.

9 Wearing a dust mask, sand off any adhesive that may have dried on the surface.

10 Attach the lamp fittings to the threaded metal rod, then conceal the rod inside the copper pipe. Attach a suitable plug to the bottom end of the flex (cord). Finally, polish the base with a soft cloth.

PURPLE CORDED LAMPSHADE

This sophisticated, one-colour design concentrates on surface texture, using slubby (textured) raw silk dupion as the background for elegant curlicues of couched silk cord that neatly echo the curly shapes of the wrought iron base.

YOU WILL NEED
paper
pencil
straight empire lampshade frame with reversible gimbal
top diameter 10cm/4in, bottom diameter 20cm/8in
and height 16cm/6¼in
scissors
self-adhesive lampshade backing material
50cm/20in purple silk dupion
tailor's chalk
purple cording
needle
matching thread
PVA (white) glue
binding tape
clothes pegs (pins)
wrought iron lamp base

1 Make a paper pattern to fit the lampshade frame you have chosen (see Techniques). Cut a piece of self-adhesive backing material to the size of the paper pattern. Cut out the purple silk, placing the pattern on the bias and adding a 1.5cm/³⁄₈in turning allowance all round.

2 Using tailor's chalk, lightly mark out freehand a swirly design on the silk piece. Remember to match up the pattern at the two ends of the fabric. Random curlicues are shown here, but you could substitute a pattern of your choice.

3 Lay the flex (cord) along the marked line. Thread a needle with matching thread and make small stitches over the flex, couching it to the silk.

4 Lay the fabric face down. Remove the paper from the backing material and position it centrally on the silk. Smooth out the fabric from the middle outwards. Apply a line of glue all round the edges of the backing material. Fold the fabric turning allowance to the wrong side and press down.

5 Wrap the frame with binding tape (see Techniques). Apply glue to the outside of the rings and the upright struts. Wrap the backed fabric around the frame. Apply a line of glue to the underside of the overlap and stick to the inner edge of the shade. Use two clothes pegs (pins) to hold the edges together until the glue is dry. Slip-stitch the folded edges in place. Spray the shade with flame retarder (retardant) if necessary (see Techniques) before fitting the shade on to the lamp base.

SPIRAL VASE

Gently spiralling bands of mosaic look very elegant on a tall vase shape. Small chips of gold smalti give extra highlights.

YOU WILL NEED
tall vase
paintbrush (optional)
yacht varnish (optional)
piece of white chalk
hammer
protective goggles
rubber (latex) gloves
marble tile
piece of sacking (heavy cloth)
cement-based tile adhesive
mixing bowl
flexible knife
glazed ceramic household tiles: pale blue and royal blue
tile nippers
gold smalti
notched spreader or cloth pad
dust mask
sandpaper
soft cloth

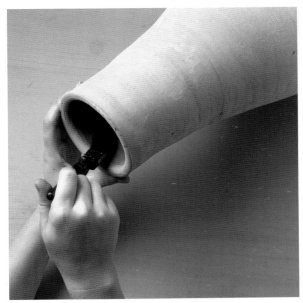

1 If your vase is unglazed, seal it by painting the inside top lip with yacht varnish.

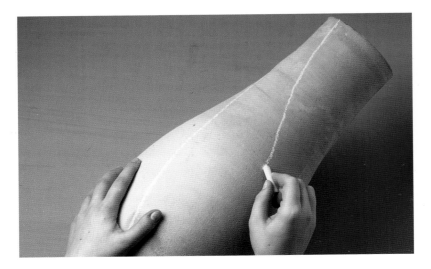

2 Using a piece of white chalk, draw lines spiralling gently from the rim of the vase to the base. Make sure you have an even number of bands and that they are regularly spaced.

3 Wearing goggles and rubber (latex) gloves, wrap the marble tile in sacking (heavy cloth) and break up into pieces with the hammer. Mix the tile adhesive according to the manufacturer's instructions. Using a flexible (putty) knife and wearing rubber gloves, spread a thin band around the top and bottom of the vase, press in the marble pieces and leave to dry overnight.

4 Using a hammer and sacking (heavy cloth) as before, and wearing the protective goggles, break up all the pale blue and royal blue tiles. Wearing rubber gloves, spread tile adhesive over the vase, a band at a time, and press in the blue tesserae (tiles), alternating the two shades. Leave until completely dry, preferably overnight.

5 Wearing goggles, cut the gold smalti into small pieces with tile nippers. Using the knife, place blobs of adhesive in the larger gaps between the blue tesserae. Press in the gold smalti pieces at random over the blue spirals, checking that they are level with the rest of the tiles. Leave to dry overnight.

6 Using a notched spreader or cloth pad, and wearing rubber gloves, rub more tile adhesive over the mosaic, filling all the gaps. Wipe off the excess and leave to dry overnight. Wearing a dust mask, sand off any adhesive dried on the surface, then polish with a soft cloth.

MAGAZINE RACK

Tidy your magazines and newspapers into this capacious rack, built from a frame of cardboard, covered with layers of papier-mâché and sponged and stencilled with silver paint against a deep blue background to resemble a starry sky.

YOU WILL NEED
pencil
metal ruler
double corrugated cardboard
craft knife
cutting mat
plate
gummed paper tape
PVA (white glue)
paintbrush
newspaper
wallpaper paste
mixing bowl
fine sandpaper
white emulsion (latex) paint
gouache paints: Prussian blue, pale gold and silver
paint-mixing container
stencil card (card stock)
sponge
acrylic spray varnish

1 Cut two rectangles from double corrugated cardboard (card stock), each measuring 40 x 30cm/16 x 12in. Draw a line 5cm/2in from one long edge of each piece, then divide this area into 5cm/2in sections. Using the edge of a plate, draw curves to join alternate upper and lower points. Cut out.

2 To make the supports, cut out two rectangles 15 x 30cm/6 x 12in, and divide them into 5cm/2in sections. Using the edge of a plate, draw concave curves to join the upper and lower points along each edge. Cut out.

3 For the ends, cut two equilateral triangles with sides of 15cm/6in and four equilateral triangles with sides of 5cm/2in. Place the two large side pieces one on top of the other, and tape along the bottom edge with gummed paper tape.

4 Place one side support on top of the side piece, aligning the lower points with the bottom edge, and tape the upper points to the side. Repeat with the other support.

5 Insert the large triangles between the sides at each end and tape in place inside and out. Insert the four small triangles between the sides and the supports at each end and tape securely. Seal the cardboard with a coat of diluted PVA (white) glue.

6 Tear newspaper into 2.5cm/1in strips and coat with wallpaper paste. Cover the whole of the magazine rack with four layers of papier-mâché. Use small pieces of paper to cover the edges and points neatly. Leave in a warm place until completely dry.

7 Rub down lightly using fine sandpaper, then prime the rack with a coat of white emulsion (latex) paint and leave to dry.

8 Using fairly dilute Prussian blue gouache, brush roughly over the whole surface and leave to dry.

9 Using pale gold gouache paint, sponge a random design all over the rack.

10 Draw a small star motif free-hand on a piece of stencil card (card stock) and cut it out using a craft knife. Sponge stars at random over the magazine rack using silver gouache paint.

11 Lightly sponge around the edges using silver gouache paint, then leave to dry completely.

12 Protect the surface of the magazine rack with a coat of acrylic spray varnish.

kitchens

For many people, the kitchen is one of the most important rooms in the home, and also one of the most versatile. It serves a variety of functions: eating, working and entertaining.

Far more than merely a place where food is prepared, the kitchen is a place where people gather and socialize as a prelude to dining. When decorating, it is therefore vital to choose a style that is conducive to relaxation and good conversation. Again, rather than purchasing expensive pieces that might look out of place in your home, concentrate on reworking what you have already got, and the results can be equally stunning.

As a place where food is prepared, the look you choose for the kitchen must be practical, but don't compromise on style. Opt for a light, informal look by decorating walls with a grape-vine motif or, alternatively, embellish your walls with a decoupage dinner set to remind everyone of what feasts lie in store. For the rustic look of the English countryside, why not make a gingham-style cushion that could complement a kitchen chair distressed with wire (steel) wool to create an aged appearance? For a more European feel, add a ribbon café curtain to your windows, or hang a bead curtain over the doorway to maximize the kitchen's natural light.

And don't forget the little details: dress up containers with glass paints that mimic stained glass, for example, or make witty fridge magnets using the technique of papier-mâché. Use your imagination, and improvements can be made almost effortlessly.

GRAPEVINE PATTERNS

This elegant repeating design is a combination of sponging and freehand painting — practise the strokes on paper before embarking on the wall, and keep your hand relaxed to make confident, sweeping lines. It's perfect for a kitchen or conservatory and is repeated on a set of glasses to carry the theme on to the table.

YOU WILL NEED
medium-density sponge, such as a household sponge
marker pen
small coin
scissors or craft knife
cutting mat
ruler
pencil
acrylic paints in purple and blue
paint-mixing container
medium and fine paintbrushes
glasses
kitchen cloth
ceramic paints in purple and blue

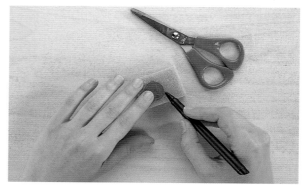

1 Copy the template at the back of the book and use to draw the leaf shape on a piece of medium-density sponge. To make the stamp for the grapes, draw around a coin, or copy the grape template.

2 Cut out the sponge shapes using a pair of scissors or craft knife.

3 Trace the template of the frieze design on to the wall, carefully marking the positions of the grapes and leaves.

4 Mix up two shades of purple acrylic paint. Using a paintbrush, load one side of the grape stamp with dark purple and the other with a lighter shade to give a shadowed effect.

5 Build up the bunch of grapes, starting with the top row and working downwards to avoid smudges. Position the grapes in succeeding rows diagonally between the ones above. Keep the dark side of each grape facing the same way.

6 Mix up two shades of blue paint and load the leaf stamp, painting the outside edge in the darker shade. Stamp the leaf shape where marked on either side of each bunch of grapes. Paint the stems free-hand in the lighter shade of blue, using a fine brush.

7 Before decorating the glasses with the grape motif, clean each thoroughly to remove any trace of grease. Leave to dry.

8 Mix two shades of purple ceramic paint and load the grape stamp as before. Align the first row of grapes below the edge of the glass, keeping clear of the rim.

9 Build up the bunch of grapes so that it fills one side of the glass.

10 Mix two shades of blue ceramic paint and load the leaf stamp as before. Stamp a leaf motif on either side of the bunch of grapes.

11 Paint the stems in the lighter shade of blue, using a fine brush. Leave the glass for 24 hours to dry completely. The glasses will withstand gentle washing but should not be put in a dishwasher or cleaned with an abrasive scourer.

FLOWERPOT FRIEZE

This witty frieze has a 1950s feel and creates an eye-catching feature above a half-boarded wall. Use scraps of leftover wallpaper or sheets of wrapping paper for the pots, and stamp an exuberant display of flowers around your kitchen.

YOU WILL NEED
matt emulsion (latex) paints in pale blue and white
broad and fine paintbrushes
old cloth
pencil
wallpaper or wrapping paper
scissors
PVA (white) glue
green acrylic paint
stamp inkpads in a variety of colours
large and small daisy rubber stamps
cotton buds (swabs)
scrap paper

1 Paint tongue-and-groove boarding or the lower half of the wall with pale blue emulsion (latex) paint and leave to dry.

2 Using a dry paintbrush, lightly brush white emulsion over the flat colour. For a softer effect, rub the paint in with an old cloth.

3 To make the frieze, draw flowerpot shapes on to scraps of different wallpapers or wrapping papers and cut them out. Cut scalloped strips of paper and glue one along the top of each flower pot, using PVA (white) glue.

4 Glue the flowerpots along the wall, at evenly spaced intervals.

5 Using acrylic paint and a fine paintbrush, paint green stems coming out of each pot. Leave the paint to dry before beginning to print the flowers.

6 Use coloured inkpads to ink the daisy stamps, using the lighter colours first. To ink the flower centre in a different colour, remove the first colour from the centre using a cotton bud (swab), then use a small inkpad to dab on the second colour.

7 Test the stamp on a sheet of scrap paper before applying it to the wall.

8 Print the lighter-coloured flowers on the ends of some of the stems, using large and small daisy stamps. Allow the ink to dry.

9 Print the darker flowers on the remaining stems. Allow the flowers to overlap to create full, blossoming pots.

WALL OF COLOUR

The colourful checkerboard wall is simply painted with sponge scourers before being embellished with cut-out plates and vases. Cheaper than buying all that china — and totally unbreakable, too, this is not a difficult design and can be attempted by a beginner.

YOU WILL NEED
PVA (white) glue
lining paper (or work directly on the wall)
medium and small paintbrushes
white emulsion (latex) paint
blue acrylic paint
two sponge scourers
pictures of plates and vases
small, sharp scissors

1 Dilute four parts PVA (white) glue with one part water. Brush on to the lining paper or wall to seal the surface.

2 Paint with white emulsion (latex) and leave to dry.

3 On a plate, mix a little blue acrylic paint into the white emulsion to make a pale blue.

4 Using two sponges, one as a spacer and the other for applying the paint, print a chequerboard pattern over the wall or paper. Practise the technique on a piece of spare paper first.

5 Make colour photocopies of pictures of plates and vases in different sizes and carefully cut them out with small, sharp scissors.

6 Arrange the photocopies on the chequered background.

7 Glue them in position with the diluted PVA (white) glue. Carefully smooth down the motifs, working from the centre to the edges.

8 Seal the finished design with the diluted PVA to protect the wall.

DRY-BRUSHED CHAIR

A soft, distressed look is achieved by dry brushing off-white paint over a light brown base painted to imitate wood. This is another excellent technique for making a tired old piece of furniture look desirably aged.

YOU WILL NEED
old cloth
sanding block and medium-grade sandpaper
pale terracotta and off-white emulsion (latex) paint
small decorator's paintbrush
sponge
matt (flat) acrylic varnish and brush

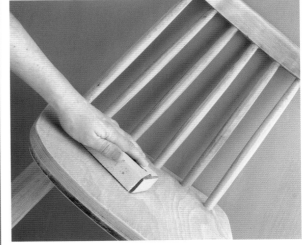

1 Wipe over the chair with a damp cloth, then sand it in the direction of the grain.

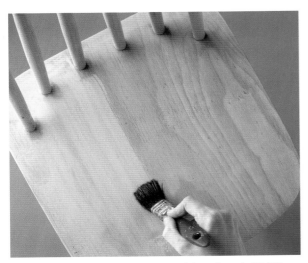

2 Mix the pale terracotta emulsion (latex) 50/50 with water. Paint the chair.

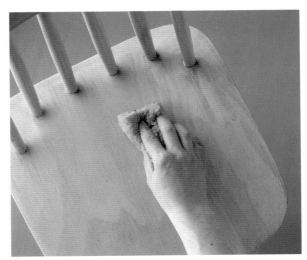

3 Using a sponge dampened with water, carefully remove the excess paint mixture.

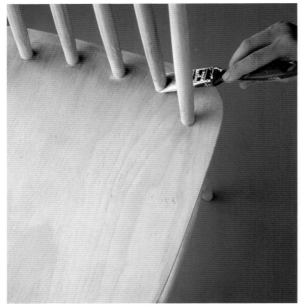

4 Using a dry brush, apply the off-white emulsion (latex) over the chair. At the angles, flick the paint from the base upwards.

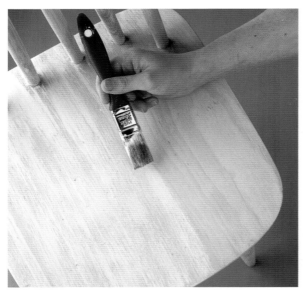

5 For the flat surfaces, hold the brush at an angle and apply the paint with minimal pressure. Seal with two coats of varnish.

SIMPLE BEAD CURTAIN

A bead curtain hung across the kitchen door is a tried and tested way to deter insects on a hot,
sunny day. This jaunty striped version is quick and cheap to make, combining wooden and
plastic beads with coloured drinking straws.

YOU WILL NEED
wire cutters
2–3 large spools of plastic-coated jewellery wire
tape measure
large, flat glass beads with central hole
large and medium plastic beads
large, medium and small wooden beads
scissors
coloured and striped plastic drinking straws
pencil
length of 2.5cm/1in wooden batten to fit inside door frame
drill
staple gun

1 Cut a length of wire to fit the door length plus 25cm/10in, and tie one end to a large glass bead, which will act as a weight at the bottom.

2 Thread on a large plastic bead between two medium wooden beads to cover the knot.

3 Using scissors, cut the drinking straws into 7.5cm/3in lengths.

4 Thread on three lengths of straw, alternating plain with striped, and threading a small wooden bead in between each.

5 Thread on a group of medium and large beads and repeat the sequence, using assorted colours, to fill the wire. Make more strands to complete the curtain.

6 Mark and drill holes at 2.5cm/1in intervals all along the batten, plus a screw hole at each end.

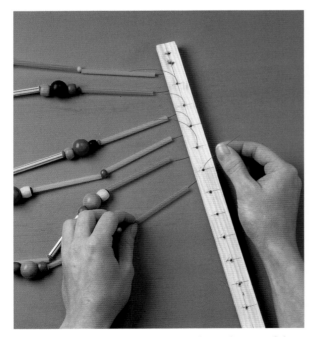

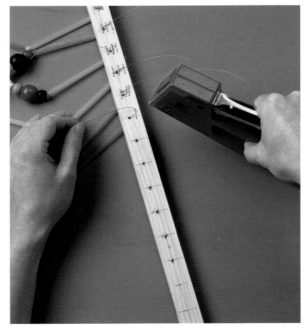

7 Thread the end of each wire through one of the holes in the batten.

8 Use a staple gun to secure the beaded threads to the batten. Attach to the door frame.

RIBBON CAFÉ CURTAIN

To dress up a small window, create this luxurious striped curtain using ribbons instead of fabric. Rows of tiny glass beads add extra sparkle to the satin; larger beads make a pretty hem and add weight to hold the ribbons straight.

YOU WILL NEED
scissors
2.5cm/1in wide satin and chiffon ribbons in toning colours
sugar
small bowl
sewing machine
matching thread
tacking (basting) thread
needle
small glass beads
large faceted plastic beads
tension rod or curtain wire to fit across window

1 Cut the ribbons to the finished length of the curtain plus 4cm/1½in. Trim one end of each ribbon length into decorative points.

2 Dissolve some sugar in a little water in a small bowl. To prevent the raw ends of the ribbon from fraying, dip the trimmed ends of each length into the solution and leave to dry.

3 Lay out enough ribbons in a repeating pattern, alternating satin and chiffon, to fit the width of the window. Using matching thread and a small zig-zag stitch, join the ribbons together. End each seam 7.5cm/3in from the bottom.

4 Fold over 3mm/⅛in then another 2.5cm/1in
along the top edge to make a casing, and tack (baste).
Starting below the casing, hand-stitch small glass
beads along each seam.

5 Thread a large plastic bead on to the end of each
satin ribbon as shown. Machine-stitch the casing
and thread the tension rod or curtain wire through it
to hang the curtain.

COUNTRY CHECK CUSHION

Patchwork and gingham go together like strawberries and cream. The patchwork front is machine-stitched for speed and strength, then hand-finished with traditional quilting knots. The cover is completed with simple ties to fasten the back.

YOU WILL NEED
stiff card (card stock)
ruler and pencil
selection of gingham fabrics
scissors
pins
tacking (basting) thread
50 cm/20 in of 90 cm-/36in wide calico
sewing thread
string
drawing pin
paper
white perle embroidery thread (floss)
tapestry needle
40 cm-/16 in-diameter cushion pad

1 Make a card (card stock) template 11cm/4¼in square. Draw around the template on to the gingham fabric and add a 1cm/½in seam allowance. Cut out 16 squares. Pin these together in pairs, with right sides facing. Stitch along one edge with a 1cm/½in seam allowance. Join the pairs into strips of four squares. Press the seams open.

2 Join two strips together along one long edge, taking care to match the seams.

3 Continue adding the strips to form a large square. Press the seams open.

4 Using the string, drawing pin and pencil, draw a 43 cm-/17 in-diameter circle on paper. Cut this out, and use it to cut a circle of calico and a circle of patchwork for the cushion front. Place the patched piece wrong side down on the calico. Tack around the edge to hold the two layers together.

5 Thread the tapestry needle with several lengths of embroidery thread (floss). Insert the needle at the corners of the patches, leaving an end of 4 cm/1½ in. Make a stitch and bring the needle back through to the right side of the fabric.

6 Tie the strands in a knot and trim. Remove the tacking (basting stitches). For the cushion back, fold the paper template vertically into four. Cut along one fold line to make one large and one small template. Cut the two back pieces from calico, adding 2.5cm/1in to each straight edge. Cut two facings 5cm/2in wide and neaten one long edge of each. Pin (tack) one facing to the smaller back piece, with right sides facing. Stitch the seam, turn and press. Stitch a hem, 2mm/1⁄16in and 2cm/¾in from the seamed edge.

7 Make six ties from 10 x 18 cm/4 x 7 in pieces of gingham (see Techniques). Position three ties at equal intervals along the opening edge of the larger back piece, matching the raw edges, and machine stitch. Pin the second facing to the opening edge, over the ties and with right sides facing, and machine stitch. Turn and fold the facing to the wrong side. Machine stitch the hem, as in step 6.

8 On the back underlap, mark the corresponding positions of the other three ties. Turn under the raw edge of each remaining tie and pin in place. Top stitch in an "X" pattern. Pin the cushion front to the backs with right sides facing, and machine stitch around the edge with a 1.5 cm/⅜ in seam. Clip the seam allowances all round. Turn right side out, insert the cushion pad and fasten the ties.

HAND-PAINTED MUGS

A set of plain-glazed earthenware mugs can be made more interesting by adding some contrasting decoration. Where the set is made of different coloured mugs, use paints that match the original colours of other mugs to make the set more harmonious. Keep the decoration at least 3cm / 1¼in below the rim for safe use, unless you intend to fire the mugs in a pottery kiln.

YOU WILL NEED
4 plain colour-glazed earthenware mugs
cleaning fluid
cloth
pencils, one with eraser tip
water-based ceramic paints in contrasting
colours plus white
paint palette
artist's paintbrushes, one fine

1 Thoroughly clean the mugs. Pencil several differently sized circles all around one of the mugs, leaving the top 5cm/2in clear. Draw the circles freehand so that they are not perfectly formed.

2 Mix up your first contrast colour, adding some white to make it opaque.

3 Fill in a circle on one of the mugs in a contrasting colour. Before the paint has dried, mark out a spiral pattern, as described in step 4.

4 Starting in the middle of the circle and using the eraser tip of a pencil, draw the spiral out to the edge. Try to do this in one movement for a neater design.

5 Paint in each remaining circle in turn, drawing out a spiral before the paint dries.

6 Using a fine paintbrush, paint radiating lines around the spirals. Leave to dry.

7 Using a fine paintbrush, paint a line detail down the outside of the handle.

8 Repeat the design on each mug, using contrasting colours, if liked.

Above: A set of mugs in different colours is given unity by matching and contrasting the painted design.

KITCHEN STORAGE JAR

*Create a decorated storage jar for holding rice, pulses or dried fruit. The frosted-look background
is etched first and then the flowers are painted in afterwards using a
selection of brightly coloured glass paints.*

YOU WILL NEED
self-adhesive vinyl
felt-tipped pen
small, sharp scissors
glass storage jar
etching paste
medium paintbrushes
rubber (latex) gloves
washing-up (dishwashing) liquid
clean cotton rag
glass paints in various colours
clear varnish

1 Decide on an overall pattern
and draw your design on to
vinyl with a felt-tipped pen.

2 Cut out the shapes carefully
using small, sharp scissors.

3 Position the shapes on to the jar and lid in an even design and press
down firmly.

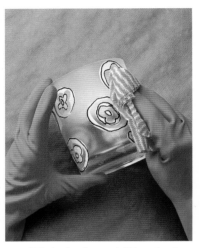

4 Wearing rubber (latex) gloves, brush a thick and even layer of etching paste over the jar and lid. Leave to dry completely.

5 Wash the jar and lid and wipe dry using a clean cotton rag.

6 Peel off the plastic shapes. If the shapes are not deeply etched enough, then repeat the process.

7 Clean off the sticky remains of the vinyl with washing-up (dishwashing) liquid and a clean cotton rag. Paint in the shapes with coloured glass paints.

8 Leave to dry, then varnish the painted areas only with the clear varnish. When the jar is completely dry, fill as desired.

FISH FRIDGE MAGNETS

Make a shoal (school) of colourful fish to swim across the door of your fridge. You can vary the thickness of the fish with the amount of papier-mâché pulp you use, but bear in mind that the more pulp applied, the longer it will take to dry.

YOU WILL NEED
pencil
stiff card (card stock)
scissors
papier-mâché pulp (see Techniques)
newspaper
PVA (white) glue
mixing bowl
fine sandpaper
white emulsion (latex) paint
paintbrush
water-soluble coloured pencils
acrylic spray varnish
epoxy resin glue
flat magnets

1 Draw a selection of fish shapes on a piece of stiff card (card stock) and cut them out using scissors.

2 Press papier-mâché pulp, about 1cm/⅓in thick, on to the fronts of the fish shapes. Leave in a warm place to dry completely.

3 Tear newspaper into 2.5cm/1in strips and soak in diluted PVA (white) glue. Cover the fish on both sides with two layers of papier-mâché. Leave to dry. ▶

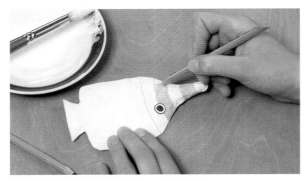

4 Lightly rub the fish down using fine sandpaper, then paint with two coats of white emulsion (latex), allowing the paint to dry between coats. When dry, decorate the fish with water-soluble coloured pencils.

5 Spray the fish on both sides with a coat of acrylic varnish. Leave to dry.

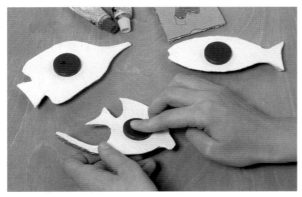

6 Using epoxy resin glue, stick a strong flat magnet to the back of each of the fish.

dining rooms

While the kitchen must be functional and designed with practicality in mind, no such restraints should apply when you reach the dining room. Here, new acquaintances can be courted and old friendships nourished, so view the dining room as a theatre for hospitality, and decorate in an altogether more extravagant manner.

First impressions count, so feel free to make bold statements here without breaking the bank. For a dramatic impression, redecorate the walls with a gothic vignette to bestow a truly grand timbre on the room. Moving to the dining table, emphasize this decadent mood by threading plain candlesticks with brilliant beads, embellishing a plain plate with a grand checkerboard motif or making a candelabra fit to grace any dining room with the simple art of papier-mâché. The ambience could be perfectly set off with a beaded night-light and an ornate napkin ring.

This chapter also contains ideas for those with more restrained tastes. For a fresh, breezy mood, why not adorn plain linen curtains with gingham-style daisies to bring summer permanently into your dining room? Accentuate the mood by placing salt and pepper shakers on the table, beautifully hand-painted to imitate the vibrant look of stained glass.

Whatever your plans, you will find that great ideas needn't cost great sums of money, and that even the smallest of changes can make all the difference.

GOTHIC WALLS

Create a dramatic setting for candlelit dinner parties with purple and gold panels that will shimmer from deep velvety green walls. The effect is achieved by stamping the wall with gold size and then rubbing on Dutch gold leaf which will adhere to the stamped motifs.

YOU WILL NEED
30cm/12in square thin card
cardboard (card stock)
ruler
pencil
scissors
high-density sponge, such as
upholstery foam (foam rubber)
marker pen
craft knife and cutting mat
matt emulsion (latex) paints in
dark green and purple
natural sponge
plumbline
small paint roller
old plate
gold size
Dutch gold leaf
soft brush

1 To make a template for the wall panels, draw a freehand arc from the centre top of the card (card stock) square to the lower corner.

2 Fold the card in half down the centre and cut out both sides to make a symmetrical Gothic arch shape.

3 Copy the design from the back of the book and make a paper pattern with a diameter of 10cm/4in. Transfer the design on to a piece of high-density sponge. Cut away the excess sponge using a craft knife.

4 Apply dark green emulsion (latex) liberally to the wall, using a sponge and working in a circular motion. Allow to dry.

5 Using a plumbline as a guide and beginning 23cm/9in from a corner, mark a vertical line up the wall to a height of 1.8m/6ft.

6 Measure across the wall and use the plumbline to draw vertical lines every 60cm/2ft.

7 Measure out 15cm/6in each side of each vertical and draw two more lines to mark the edges of the panels.

8 Place the point of the card (card stock) template at the centre top point of each panel and draw in the curves.

9 Use a small paint roller to load the stamp with gold size and print each panel, beginning with the centre top and working down the central line, then down each side.

10 When the size is tacky, apply Dutch gold leaf by rubbing over the backing paper with a soft brush.

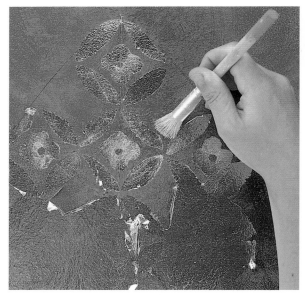

11 Once the panel is complete, use a soft brush to remove any excess gold leaf.

12 Using only the centre of the stamp, fill in the spaces between the gold motifs using purple emulsion (latex) paint.

APPLIQUED GINGHAM CURTAIN

*Though charmingly rustic and fresh looking, black-and-white gingham makes a smart,
crisp trimming for a neutral linen curtain. Arrange the flowers at varying heights
to give the impression that they are growing up from the hem.*

YOU WILL NEED

tape measure

scissors

plain linen fabric

iron

sewing machine

matching thread

gingham

needle

pins

tracing paper

pencil

fusible bonding web

small amounts of plain and gingham fabrics

1 Measure the width of the curtain pole and decide on the length of the curtain. Cut the fabric to one and a half times the width and add 10cm/4in to the length for seam allowances. Turn in and press a 1cm/½in double hem down both side edges and a 5cm/2in double hem along the bottom edge. Machine-stitch all three hems.

2 Calculate the number of ties needed, spacing them about 20cm/8in apart. For each tie, cut a piece of gingham 6 x 40cm (2½ x 16in). Fold in half lengthways, right sides together. Stitch along the length, press the seam to the centre and stitch across one end. Trim and turn right side out. Tuck in the raw edges and slip-stitch the remaining end.

3 Turn over and press to the right side a 1cm/½in single hem at the top of the curtain. Fold the ties in half widthways and pin the folded ends to the top edge of the curtain on the right side, spacing them evenly. Machine-stitch in place.

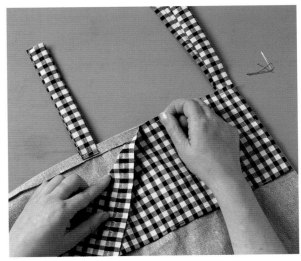

4 To make the heading, cut a 14cm/5½in strip of gingham to the width of the curtain plus 4cm/1½in. Fold and press a 2cm/¾in turning on all sides of the strip.

5 Lay the heading along the top edge of the curtain, matching the folded edges, and pin in position. Machine-stitch all round the heading.

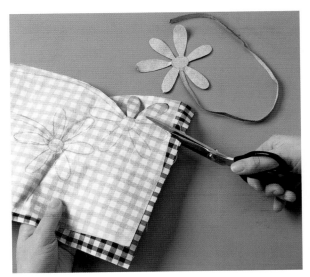

6 Scale up the daisy template at the back of the book. Trace as many flower shapes as you will need on to a piece of fusible bonding web and cut out roughly. Lay the shapes, sticky side down, on a selection of plain and gingham fabrics. Press to fuse them in place. Cut the motifs out carefully.

7 Peel away the paper backing and arrange the flower motifs across the hem of the curtain. When you are happy with the design, press to fuse them in place.

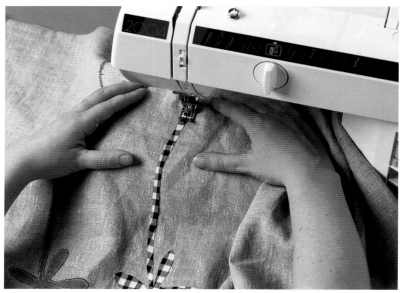

8 Machine-stitch around each flower motif, using straight stitch, keeping as close to the edge of the motif as possible.

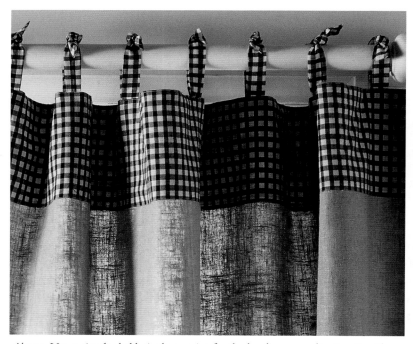

Above: Use a simple, bold gingham print for the heading, co-ordinating it with cushions and table settings for a pretty overall effect.

CANDLE SHADES

These delicate-looking shades, made from Japanese handmade paper and photocopies of real leaves and flowers, match the soft glow of candlelight. They are treated with fire-proofing spray, but for extra safety, do not leave them unattended when lit.

YOU WILL NEED
Japanese handmade paper
clear oil-based dead-flat varnish
medium and small paintbrushes
pair of compasses (compass)
ruler
pencil
card (card stock)
scissors
selection of fresh and dried flowers
and leaves
craft knife
cutting mat
masking tape
wallpaper paste or PVA (white) glue
decorative paper
fire-proofing spray (fire retardant)
candle
candlestick

1 Varnish the handmade paper with clear dead-flat varnish and leave to dry.

2 Using a pair of compasses (compass), a ruler and a pencil, draw the shape of the shade on to card (card stock), following the design shown overleaf. Cut out the design to use as a template.

3 Draw around the card template on to the handmade paper and cut out.

4 Make colour photocopies of the flowers and leaves. Carefully cut them out using a craft knife and cutting mat.

5 To plan your design, arrange the cut-outs on the handmade paper, securing them temporarily with masking tape. Glue them in place.

6 Cut out edging details from strips of decorative paper and glue them in place. Leave space at the joining edge. Once the shade is made up, you can add extra pieces to cover the join.

7 Cover the shade with a coat of clear varnish. Leave to dry, then glue the shade together.

8 Draw around the larger circumference on a piece of card to make the shade support.

9 In the centre of the support, draw a smaller circle for the candle to fit through. Draw intersecting lines through this circle. Then mark four more holes to allow air to circulate. Cut out the support and the small circles.

10 Spray the shade and card (card stock) with fire-proofing (fire retardant) spray.

11 Push the candle through the card support on to the candlestick. Place the shade over the candle to rest on the support.

CHECKERBOARD DINNER PLATE

Like so many successful designs, this stunning dinner plate owes its impact to its simplicity.
A table set with several of these plates would look just wonderful. You can create a set
in a matter of minutes.

YOU WILL NEED
plain white china plate
cleaning fluid
cloth
sponge
craft knife or scalpel
water-based enamel paints: blue,
green and yellow
paper towel
masking fluid
artist's paintbrushes
cotton buds (swabs)

1 Clean the plate. Cut several cubes of sponge for sponging the paint on to the plate. Holding the sponge taut as you slice a square down into the sponge will make cutting easy and the lines straight. Load the first sponge cube with blue paint and dab the plate to make a checkerboard pattern. Let dry.

2 Load a second sponge with green paint and dab it in the gaps between the blue squares.

3 Use a damp paper towel to wipe off any excess paint on the rim of the plate.

4 Paint a decorative border design around the rim of the plate with masking fluid and leave to dry.

5 Sponge blue paint all over the rim of the plate, leaving a narrow border around the central squares. Leave until the paint is dry.

6 Gently rub off the dried masking fluid with a damp paper towel to reveal the painted design.

7 Use yellow paint to highlight the design around the border, tidying up the design with cotton buds (swabs), if necessary. The plate should be fired in a pottery kiln before use.

BEADED WIRE CANDLESTICKS

Twisted silver wire, sparingly threaded with beads, has a delicate yet sculptural quality. An assortment of decorative glass beads, following a colour theme, attracts the light and looks wonderful entwining a pair of glass candlesticks.

YOU WILL NEED
tape meaure
wire cutters
medium silver wire
pair of glass candlesticks
round-nosed jewellery pliers
medium decorative glass beads in yellow, green,
silver and clear
pen or pencil
small glass rocaille beads and square beads in
complementary shades

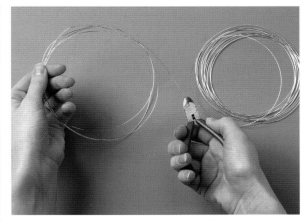

1 Cut four 1m/39in lengths of medium silver wire for each candlestick.

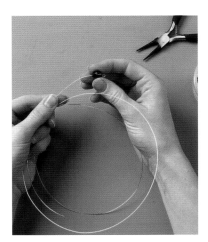

2 Bend a loop at the end of the first length and thread on a decorative bead.

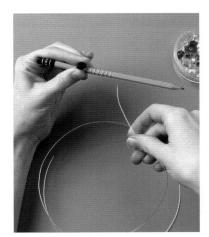

3 Wind the end of the wire around a pen or pencil six times to form a spiral.

4 Thread on about eight small glass beads and divide them among the loops. Thread on another medium-sized bead and repeat, forming spirals and threading beads until you reach the end ▶ of the wire.

5 When you reach the end of the wire, use the pliers to twist the end.

6 Thread on the final decorative bead and finish with a loop at the end of the wire.

7 Make up the other three spirals in the same way, distributing the coloured beads evenly among the loops.

8 Wrap two spiral lengths around the stem of each candlestick to form an interesting shape. Secure the spirals in place by binding them gently to the stem with more wire.

GOTHIC CANDELABRA

As if rooted in the base of this graceful candelabra, sinuous ivy entwines its stem and arms.
The basic structure consists of wire coathangers and some cardboard, coated with several layers
of newspaper, and handmade paper to add weight and tensile strength.

YOU WILL NEED
pliers
3 wire coathangers
jam jar
pencil
pair of compasses (compass)
ruler
heavy corrugated cardboard
craft knife
cutting mat
thin garden wire
gummed paper tape
thin card (card stock)
newspaper
PVA (white) glue
mixing bowl
handmade paper
masking tape
papier-mâché pulp (see Techniques)
paintbrushes
fine sandpaper
acrylic varnish
acrylic paints
paint-mixing container

1 Using pliers, bend two wire coathangers to make two curved arms for the candelabra. Bend the wire around a jam jar to get a smooth shape. Cut the hooks off the hangers.

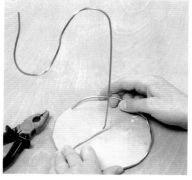

2 Draw a 15 cm/6 in diameter circle on heavy corrugated cardboard and cut it out. Using pliers and a jam jar again, bend the lower end of each wire arm into a semicircle to fit around the edge of the cardboard and reinforce the base.

3 Assemble the structure, binding the two arms together with thin garden wire to make the stem. Attach the cardboard base to the wires with gummed paper tape.

4 To make the candle-holders, cut two 9cm/3½in circles of thin card (card stock). Make a slit to the centre of each and twist them into cone shapes. Secure with tape. Soak newspaper strips in diluted PVA (white) glue and cover the cones with a layer of papier-mâché. Push them on to the ends of the wire arms and secure with tape.

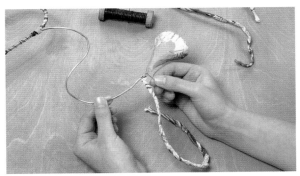

5 Twist long strips of newspaper and wrap them around the wire frame. Secure the twists with thin garden wire.

6 Soak strips of handmade paper in diluted PVA glue and cover the structure with a layer of papier-mâché.

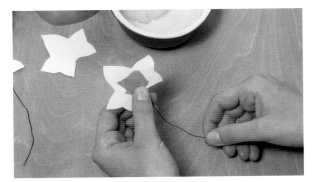

7 Bend a third wire coathanger to make the stem of the ivy. Draw 8–10 ivy leaf shapes on thin card, cut out and tape each one to a short length of thin garden wire.

8 Use the thin wire stalks to attach the leaves to the ivy stem and secure with masking tape. Cover the ivy stem and stalks with handmade paper strips.

▶

9 Using thin garden wire, attach the ivy stem to the main frame. Twist the stem around the candelabra in an attractive shape and wire it in place.

10 Cover the whole candelabra in a layer of papier-mâché pulp. Leave to dry completely in a warm place.

11 Use fine sandpaper to smooth the papier-mâché, taking care not to disturb the shape of the candelabra.

12 Spray the candelabra with a coat of acrylic varnish to seal it. Decorate with gold and silver gouache paints and varnish again.

NAPKIN RING AND NIGHT-LIGHT

Wired rocaille beads, woven into simple striped designs, shimmer in the candlelight and make delicate yet sumptuous ornaments for the dinner table. It is essential to use a night-light with its own metal container in the night-light holder.

YOU WILL NEED
fine galvanized wire
ruler or tape measure
wire cutters
round-nosed jewellery pliers
plastic bottle and beaker, to use as formers
glass rocaille beads in pink, red and orange
fine silver wire
adhesive pads

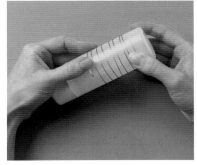

1 For the napkin ring, take about 2m/78in of galvanized wire and bend a small loop in one end using pliers. Wind the wire about ten times around the plastic bottle or beaker.

2 Thread enough pink glass rocaille beads onto the wire to fit around the bottle or beaker once, then change to red and thread another round of beads.

3 Go on threading beads in this sequence until the wire is full, then use the pliers to bend another small loop in the end to prevent the beads falling off.

4 Bend the beaded wire around the bottle or beaker again to restore its shape. Secure a length of fine silver wire to the first row, then bind it around the others, keeping the spiral in shape. Do this at two or three other points around the napkin ring.

5 When the ring is complete, wind the ends of the silver wires back around the previous rows to neaten, and snip off the excess.

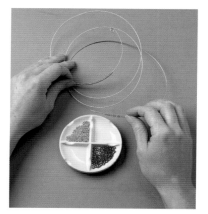

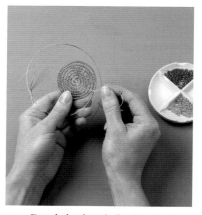

6 To make the night-light holder, bend one end of a long piece of galvanized wire into a small loop as before. Thread the first part of the wire with orange glass rocailles.

7 Bend the beaded wire into a small spiral to form the base of the night-light holder. Attach two lengths of silver wire to the centre of the spiral and bind each row to the previous one to secure the shape. Thread on more beads if necessary until the base fits that of the plastic bottle or beaker.

8 Use adhesive pads to attach the beaded spiral base temporarily to the base of the bottle or beaker.

9 Join on more galvanized wire if necessary, by twisting the ends together with pliers. Then thread on enough orange rocailles to wind around the bottle or beaker about four or five times.

10 Wind the beaded wire around the bottle or beaker, binding each row to the last using the silver wire. Pull the wire quite tight to hold the shape.

11 Change to the red beads and repeat until the holder reaches the height you want. To finish, bind the silver wire a few times tightly around the beaded wire and back around the previous rows. Snip off the ends.

SALT AND PEPPER SHAKERS

Create a conversation piece at mealtimes with matching salt and pepper shakers. Look in kitchenware and charity shops for plain glass items to decorate, and add as much or as little decoration as you like.

YOU WILL NEED
glass salt and pepper shakers
contour relief paint in black and gold
glass paints in various colours
medium paintbrushes
clear varnish

1 Draw a few loose circles on to the shakers with black contour relief paint.

2 When the lines are dry, colour in the background with glass paint.

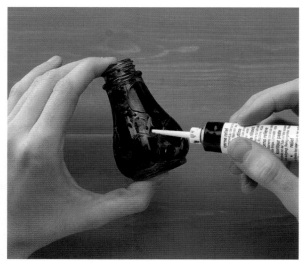

3 Fill in the circles with a different coloured paint or a variety of different colours.

4 Apply dots of black contour paint over the background colour to add texture.

109

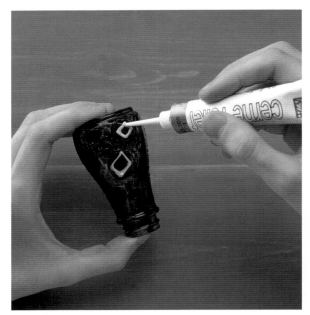

5 When dry, paint squares over the circles using the gold contour relief paint.

6 Leave the shakers to dry for at least 4 hours, then paint with clear varnish.

bedrooms

The bedroom is the one room in the house where you can give in to your every whim. It is perhaps the only room in your home where practicality need not be a prime consideration, and fantasy can take over. Whatever your dreams, from the exotic to the regal, the bedroom is the perfect place for relaxing and letting go.

For those who want a truly extravagant look, why not paint your walls a dramatic pink? You might also like to use materials outside of their traditional context – twist convention by using silk in vibrant colours embellished with ribbons to create an eye-catching window dressing. If you yearn for a look that is high on romance, why not adorn your bedroom in dreamy lilac stripes?

Remember too that while it is all too easy to concentrate on extensive changes to create a dramatic first impression, it is the small details that bring a personal touch to a room. Even a small bedroom can support well-chosen accessories - a tiny posy on a bedside table, a basket of old-fashioned pomanders, or a freshly laundered pile of bed linen.

Transform overlooked light sources into eye-catching ornaments and dress up a lampshade with flowers and leaves. Embellish a plain wall sconce with gold paint and an array of beads to create a focal point. For softer lighting, fashion a dramatic candle-holder in intense, dramatic stained glass.

Remember, your bedroom is your own private haven - so indulge your decorating whims, simply because you can!

MISTY LILAC STRIPES

Here, wide stripes are painted and the wet paint dabbed with mutton cloth (stockinet) to soften the effect and blend in brushmarks. Careful measuring is required, but it is worth the effort. As an extra touch, paint a triangle at the top of each stripe. If you do not have a picture rail, take the stripes up to the top of the wall and place the triangles along the skirting board (baseboard).

YOU WILL NEED
white silk finish emulsion (latex) paint
paint roller and tray
ruler and pencil
plumbline
masking tape
lilac emulsion (latex) paint
acrylic scumble
medium decorator's paintbrush
mutton cloth (stockinet)
small piece of card (card stock)
scissors
paint guard or strip of card (cardboard)

1 Paint the walls white, using a paint roller and tray. Mark the centre of the most important wall, below the picture rail (if you have one), with a pencil. Make marks 7.5cm/3in on either side of this, then every 15cm/6in. Continue around the room until the marks meet at the least noticeable corner.

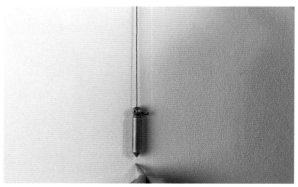

2 Hang a short length of plumbline from one of the marks, and mark with a dot where it rests. Hang the plumbline from this dot and mark where it rests. Continue down the wall. Repeat for each mark below the picture rail.

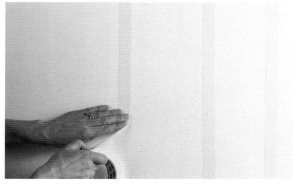

3 Starting in the centre of the wall, place strips of masking tape either side of the marked row of dots to give a 15cm/6in wide stripe. Repeat for the other rows of dots.

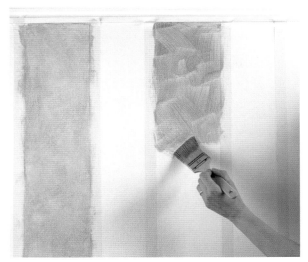

4 Dilute some of the lilac paint with about 25% water and 25% acrylic scumble. Brush on to a section of the first stripe. Complete each stripe in two or three stages, depending on the height of the room, blending the joins to get an even result.

5 Dab the wet paint lightly with a mutton cloth (stockinet) to smooth out the brushmarks. Complete all the stripes, then carefully peel away the masking tape and leave the paint to dry.

6 Cut a card (card stock) triangle with a 15cm/ 6in base and measuring 10cm/4in from the base to the tip. Use this as a template to mark the centre of each of the stripes, lilac and white, 10cm/ 4in below the picture rail.

7 Working on one stripe at a time, place strips of masking tape between the top corners of the stripe and the marked dot, as shown.

▶

8 Brush on the lilac paint mix, then dab the mutton cloth (stockinet) over the wet paint as before. Leave the paint to dry. Repeat for all the stripes.

9 Dilute some lilac paint with about 20 parts water. Brush over the wall in all directions to give a hint of colour to the white stripes.

10 Add a little paint to the remaining diluted mixture to strengthen the colour. Using a paint guard or strip of card (cardboard) to protect the painted wall, brush the paint on to the picture rail.

HOT PINK WALL

Here, pure powder pigment is mixed with neutral wax to achieve maximum colour intensity, quite unlike paint. The colour is worked in with vertical strokes to give a rough, dragged effect, which would look very striking in a contemporary setting.

YOU WILL NEED
magenta powder pigment
neutral wax
bowl
protective gloves
small decorator's paintbrush
old cloths

1 Mix one part magenta powder pigment to two parts wax in a bowl. Put on protective gloves.

2 Using a paintbrush, drag the mixture down the wall.

3 Using a cloth, rub the colour into the wall surface. Repeat over the rest of the wall.

Above: In this alternative colourway, violet powder pigment has been mixed with the wax.

STAINED GLASS SCREEN

In this project the mosaic is laid on top of clear glass. Place the screen in front of a window by day or a glowing fire at night so that the light shines through.

YOU WILL NEED
mitre block
tape measure
hacksaw
3 pieces of 2.5cm/1in x 3.5cm/1½in
wood, each 206cm/82½in long, with a
1cm/½in rebate
wood glue
hammer
12 corner staples
dark pencil
hand drill
4 small hinges
screwdriver
screws
large sheet of paper
black marker pen
3 pieces of clear glass, each 70 x 25cm/
28 x 10in
indelible marker pen
glass cutter
protective goggles
7 pieces of coloured glass,
27cm/10½in square
clear all-purpose adhesive
tile grout
universal black stain
rubber (latex) gloves
mixing bowl
old toothbrush
paint scraper
soft cloth
3 pieces of rectangular beading, each
2m/78in long
panel pins (brads)
12 metal corner plates

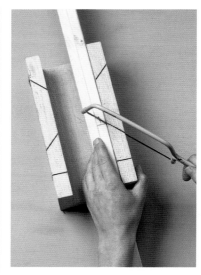

1 Using a mitre block and a hacksaw, cut six pieces of rebated wood 74cm/29in long. Cut six more lengths of rebated wood each 29cm/11½in long. These will form the wooden frame for the screen.

2 Lay the pieces of wood out on a flat surface to make three oblong frames. Glue the mitred ends together with wood glue, checking they are at right angles. Leave to dry, then hammer in a corner staple at each corner.

3 Place one frame on top of another, with the rebates facing outwards. With a pencil, mark the position of two hinges and their screwholes as shown. Using a hand drill, make a shallow guidehole for each screw, then screw in the hinges. Attach the third frame in the same way to form a three-piece screen.

4 Place the three frames face down on a large sheet of paper. Using a marker pen, draw around the inner edge of each frame. Draw a simple design that flows in bands of colour from one frame to the next.

5 Place the pieces of clear glass over the paper drawing — the glass will be slightly larger. Using an indelible pen, trace your design on to the glass, taking care not to press too hard against it.

6 Using a glass cutter and wearing protective goggles, cut 12 right-angled triangles of coloured glass (see Techniques) for the corners of the screen. Reserve on one side. Cut the rest into random pieces.

7 Using clear adhesive, glue the coloured pieces on to the clear glass panels. Work on a section of your design at a time, following each band across to the other panels. Leave to dry for 2 hours.

8 Mix the tile grout with the black stain and rub over the surface of the mosaic – it is advisable to wear rubber (latex) gloves. Use a toothbrush to make sure all the gaps are filled. Leave to dry for 1 hour.

9 When completely dry, clean off the excess grout. Residual, stubborn grout can be carefully removed with a paint scraper. Finish removing any smaller areas of grout with a soft cloth.

10 Glue one of the reserved right-angled triangles of coloured glass over the corner of the frames, at the front. Repeat with the other triangles, on each corner of the frame.

11 Cut the beading into six 71cm/28in lengths and six 23cm/9in lengths. Place the glass panels in the frames, slot the beading behind them and fix with panel pins (narrow-headed nails).

12 Make shallow guideholes with a hand drill, then screw the corner plates to the back of each corner of the frame. Finally, polish the surface of the mosaic screen with a soft cloth.

RIBBON FLOWER CURTAINS

Sheer curtains don't have to be white: choose a fabric in a vibrant shade and add an assortment
of equally bright ribbons, coiled into flowers, to decorate your window with a riot of colour.
A wider ribbon forms the casing at the top.

YOU WILL NEED
tape measure
scissors
sheer fabric
tailor's chalk
embroidery hoop
tacking (basting) thread
needle
9mm/³⁄₈in wide satin ribbons in assorted colours
sewing machine
matching threads
iron
self-cover buttons
scraps of coloured fabrics
easy button cover
4cm/1¹⁄₂in wide satin ribbon
pins

1 Measure the window and decide on the finished length of the curtain. Cut the fabric to length, adding 4cm/1¹⁄₂in for seam allowances. The fabric should be at least one-and-a-half times the width of the window. Lay out the fabric on a flat surface and decide where you want to stitch the flowers. Mark each position with tailor's chalk. Fit an embroidery hoop over the first marked point.

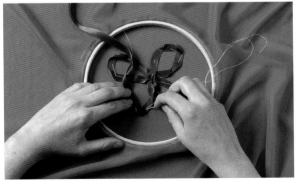

2 Tack (baste) a length of 9mm/³⁄₈in wide ribbon in the shape of a flower on to the fabric inside the embroidery hoop. Cut off the excess ribbon.

3 Machine-stitch the flower in place, then coil a length of contrasting ribbon in the centre and stitch. Make the other flowers in different coloured ribbons.

▶

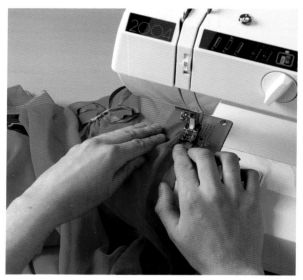

4 Fold and press 1cm/½in double hems all round the fabric. Machine-stitch.

5 Cover some self-cover buttons with scraps of fabric in assorted colours. Use an easy button cover to speed up the process.

6 Cut a piece of 4cm/1½in ribbon to the width of the curtain plus 2cm/¾in. Hand-stitch the buttons, evenly spaced, in a line along the centre.

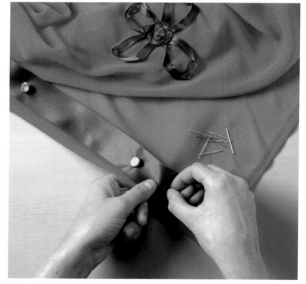

7 Fold over the ends of the ribbon so that it fits the width of the curtain and pin it in place 1cm/½in below the top edge. Machine-stitch along each side of the ribbon to make a casing for the curtain wire.

TIMELESS CUSHION

Perfect as a christening gift or to celebrate the birth of a baby, this delicate cushion in fresh gingham and broderie anglaise has timeless appeal. Photocopy your chosen initials — calligraphy books are always a good source of attractive lettering — ready to transfer to the fabric.

YOU WILL NEED
12.5 cm/5 in square of 12-count
aida fabric
sewing thread
soft pencil
stranded embroidery thread (floss)
vanishing fabric marker
15 x 17 cm/6 x 6½ in gingham
33 cm/13 in narrow white broderie
anglaise edging
1.5 m/1¾ yd of 10 cm-/4 in-wide broderie
anglaise edging
15 x 17 cm/6 x 7 in white backing fabric
polyester stuffing
pot-pourri
four buttons

1 Find the centre of the aida fabric by folding it in half each way and tacking (basting) along the creases. Transfer your chosen initials to the fabric, and sew them in cross stitch so that one initial lies on each side of the central line.

2 Cut a 10 cm/4 in square of paper. Place this diagonally on the embroidery so that one corner lies on each tacked line. Draw around it with a vanishing fabric marker and cut out the diamond shape.

3 Pin (tack) and stitch the diamond shape to the centre of the gingham. Slip stitch the narrow broderie anglaise around the diamond, mitring it neatly at the corners (see Techniques).

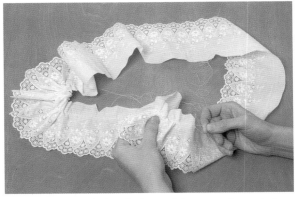

4 Join the wide broderie anglaise to make a circle. Fold this into four, and mark the quarters with notches on the top edge. Make four lines of gathering stitches, by hand or machine, between the notches (see Techniques).

127

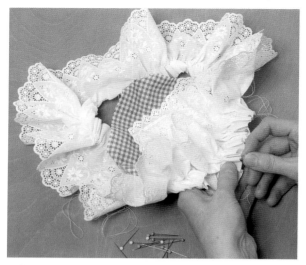

5 Pin (tack) one notch to each corner of the gingham, so that the lace lies towards the centre. Draw up the gathering threads so that the frill fits along each side, and knot the thread ends. Distribute the gathers evenly, allowing a little more fullness at each corner. Pin and tack (baste) in place.

6 Pin the gathers to the gingham, so that they do not get caught in the stitching. With right sides facing, pin the gingham front to the white backing fabric. Stitch them together 1 cm/½ in from the edge, leaving a 5 cm/2 in gap on one side.

7 Clip the corners and turn the cover right side out. Stuff with stuffing and pot-pourri, then slip stitch the opening closed.

8 Finish by sewing a button on to each corner of the cushion with embroidery thread (floss).

BEADED CUSHION TRIMS

Although these cushion trims appear very delicate, they are stitched along the seams using a strong thread and are unlikely to break. Part of the fun is experimenting with designs: drops and swags always look stunning.

YOU WILL NEED
150cm/60in each purple and green linen
scissors
tape measure
pins
sewing machine
matching thread
two cushion pads, one 35cm/14in square and
30cm/12in square
graph paper
pencil
fine beading needle
strong non-stretch bead thread
iridescent beads in pink and green
rocaille beads in gold, silver and red
frosted bugle beads in pink, blue and green
green metallic bugle beads
small crystal beads in pink, blue and yellow

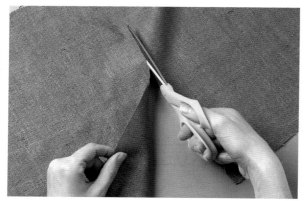

1 First make up the cushion covers. Cut a 38cm/15in square from the purple linen for the front of the larger cushion, and two pieces for the back measuring 38 x 28cm/15 x 11in. For the smaller cushion, cut a 33cm/13in square and two back pieces measuring 33 x 23cm/13 x 9in.

2 Stitch a narrow hem across one long edge of each back piece. Place both of these pieces on top of the front piece, right sides together, overlapping the hemmed edges at the centre. Stitch all round the covers with a 1.5cm/⅝in seam allowance and turn right-side out. Insert the cushion pads.

3 Decide on the design of the trim, drawing your ideas on a piece of graph paper.

4 The trim for the purple cushion is made up of alternate swags and drops and is stitched along two opposite edges of the cushion. Measure one edge of the cushion and divide it at equidistant points approximately 5cm/2in apart. Mark each point vertically with a pin.

5 Begin the trim at the left-hand edge, starting with the beads along the seam to help mark out the position of the swags and drops. Make a small fastening stitch, then thread up an iridescent pink bead followed by a gold rocaille. Take the needle around the last bead, then back through the pink bead, into the cushion seam and back out along the seam beside the pink bead.

6 Thread up a line of pink frosted bugle beads alternating with gold rocaille beads. Take a stitch through the seam about halfway along the line and continue until you reach the first marker pin. Thread up a green iridescent bead followed by a gold rocaille bead in the same manner as for the pink bead. Continue until the line of beads along the seam is complete.

7 The drops and swags can be completed together. Thread up the first drop, inserting the needle just below the pink iridescent bead. Thread up a silver rocaille followed by a blue frosted bugle and repeat. Follow with a silver rocaille, a pink crystal and a silver rocaille. Take the needle around the last bead and back up through the rest. Return the needle through the seam line, fasten off and bring it out one bead to the right.

8 Continue with the swag. Thread a silver rocaille followed by a frosted bugle and repeat twice; thread another silver rocaille, a gold rocaille and a pink crystal. Repeat the beads on the other side of the crystal as a mirror image. Stitch into the seam line and fasten off just under the green iridescent bead. Continue with alternate drops and swags until the trim is complete.

9 The green cushion trim is made up of alternating drops and triangles. Use the same method as before to mark out the seam line with pins, this time at 3cm/1¼in intervals.

10 Follow the same method as before, but start with the drops and triangles. Thread up the first drop consisting of two red rocailles, a blue frosted bugle, a red rocaille, a green frosted bugle, red rocaille, blue frosted bugle, red rocaille, blue crystal and red rocaille. Take the needle around the last bead and back up through the rest. Fasten off and bring the needle out one bead along.

11 Continue with the triangle. Thread a single red rocaille followed by the same configuration of beads as for the drop. Then, instead of a blue crystal, thread a yellow crystal followed by a red rocaille. This time take the needle around the last bead, back up through the crystal bead only and continue threading the other side of the triangle as a mirror image of the first side. Attach to the seam just to the left of the pin marker, fasten off and continue with alternate drops and triangles until complete.

12 Stitch a line of beads along the seam line, in the gaps left by the triangles. Insert the needle and thread up a gold rocaille, green metallic bugle, three gold rocailles, another bugle and finally a gold rocaille. Stitch at the marker to fasten, then continue until you reach the end of the seam.

STAINED GLASS CANDLE-HOLDER

Squares of coloured glass cast beautiful patterns at night, when the candle is lit in a darkened room. Practise the glass-cutting technique first on scraps of clear glass.

YOU WILL NEED
pencil
ruler
graph paper
sheets of textured coloured glass
glass cutter
pliers
protective goggles
clear all-purpose adhesive
clear glass candle-holder
white tile grout
mixing bowl
flexible (putty) knife
rubber (latex) gloves
sponge or soft cloth

1 Using a pencil and ruler, draw a grid of 4cm/1½in squares on graph paper.

2 Place each sheet of coloured glass over the grid. Following your drawn lines, score vertical lines with a glass cutter (see Techniques).

3 Using pliers and wearing goggles, snap the glass along the scored lines (see Techniques) into neat, evenly sized pieces.

135

4 Place each strip of glass over the paper grid, score horizontal lines and snap off the squares, until you have enough squares to cover the candle-holder.

5 Stick the squares of glass in neat rows around the candle-holder with clear glue, alternating the colours, and leaving a tiny gap in between each tile.

6 Mix the tile grout as recommended by the manufacturer. Using a flexible (putty) knife, spread over the surface of the candle-holder, filling all the gaps between the squares. It is advisable to wear rubber (latex) gloves. Rub the excess grout off the surface with a damp sponge or soft cloth. Leave to dry completely, then polish with a dry soft cloth before using.

FLOWERS AND LEAVES LAMPSHADE

Perfect for a romantically decorated bedroom, this delicate silk lampshade is scattered with tiny flowers. The leaves, cut from the same fabric as the shade, are stitched on to the silk before backing. Glossy satin binding completes the design.

YOU WILL NEED
paper
pencil
straight empire lampshade frame
with reversible gimbal, top diameter
10cm/4in, bottom diameter 20cm/8in, height 16cm/6¼in
scissors
self-adhesive lampshade backing
material
50cm/20in white silk dupion
iron
fusible bonding web
card (card stock) for template
embroidery scissors
sewing machine
matching thread
PVA (white) glue
artificial flowers
satin bias binding (tape)
glue gun
clothes pegs (pins)
needle
wooden lamp base
fine-grade sandpaper
white acrylic paint
paintbrush

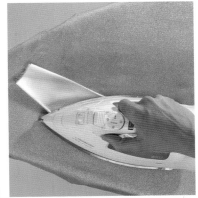

1 Make a paper pattern to fit the frame you have chosen (see Techniques). Cut a piece of self-adhesive backing material to the size of the paper pattern. Carefully cut out the silk fabric, placing the pattern on the bias and adding a 1.5cm/⅝in turning allowance all round. Fold the fabric in half three times, and press in the folds with an iron to mark eight sections.

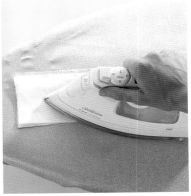

2 Cut a piece of fusible bonding web 15 x 7.5cm/ 6 x 3in and a piece of white silk to the same size. Lay the bonding web on a flat surface, adhesive side down on the wrong side of the silk, and fuse in place with an iron. Be careful to follow the manufacturer's instructions on the bonding web for the temperature setting on your iron or you may scorch the silk.

3 Copy the leaf design from the back of the book and make a template from stiff, thick card (card stock). Draw around the template on to the backing paper 16 times. Cut out the leaf shapes carefully, using a pair of small, sharp embroidery scissors.

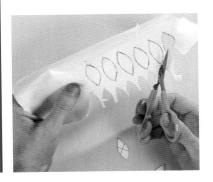

4 Open out the silk. Peel away the backing paper from each leaf shape and arrange a pair of leaves on either side of each fold line in the silk, 5cm/2in from the fabric edge, alternately at the top and bottom of the shade or according to your own design. Fuse in place with an iron. Again, take care to set the iron to the correct temperature as recommended by the manufacturer of the backing fabric.

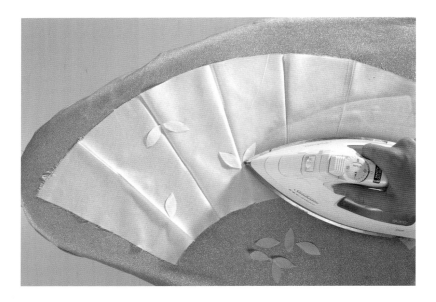

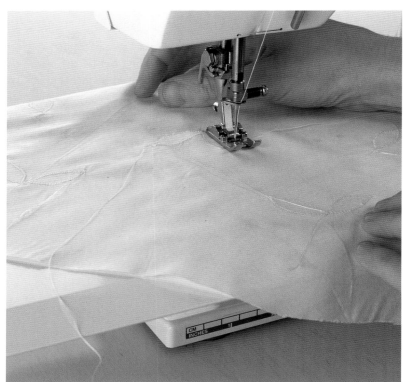

5 Setting your sewing machine to zig-zag mode, work a narrow zig-zag stitch around each shape using matching thread.

6 Lay the appliquéd fabric face down and position the large piece of backing material in the centre. Smooth out the fabric from the middle outwards. Turn in and glue the fabric allowance (see Techniques). Snip the artificial flowers from their stems. Apply a small blob of PVA (white) glue to each flower and stick a neat row along the top edge of the shade. Stick a flower in the middle of each pair of leaves.

7 Cut a piece of satin bias binding (tape) the length of the bottom edge of the silk plus 2cm/³⁄₄in. Using the glue gun, apply a line of glue or PVA (white) glue to the bottom edge of the shade and press one long edge of the binding to the edge of the silk. Turn the other long edge to the inside and glue to the shade in the same way. Leave to dry completely before proceeding to the next step.

8 Apply a line of glue along the underside of one side edge, roll the shade into a cone and lap (press) the glued edge over the opposite edge. Use two clothes pegs (pins) to hold the edge firmly together until the glue is dry. Check that the cover fits the frame. Slip-stitch the folded edges. Apply lines of glue around the outside edges of the frame and insert the frame into the cover.

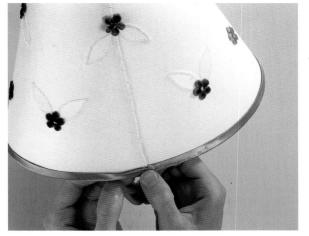

9 Stick the rest of the artificial flowers along the top edge to obsure the seam of the shade, and between the final pair of leaves. Leave to dry completely.

10 Where the ends of the bias binding meet, turn under 1cm/½in of one raw end and stick it down with a blob of glue so that it overlaps the other raw end. Use two clothes pegs (pins) to hold the ends firmly until the glue is dry.

11 Rub down the wooden lamp base with fine-grade sandpaper to remove the varnish or any other finish.

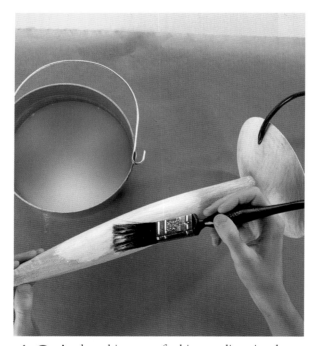

12 Apply a thin coat of white acrylic paint, leave to dry thoroughly, then rub down again to create a distressed effect. Spray the shade with flame retarder (retardant) if necessary and dry completely. Attach the base to the shade and use a low-wattage bulb for a romantic bedside glow.

BEADED WALL SCONCE

French-style beaded chandeliers or wall sconces are beautiful but expensive. However, it's easy to create your own: transform a junk shop or fleamarket find with the help of gold paint, wire and swags of cheap but effective plastic crystal beads.

YOU WILL NEED
wall sconce
metallic gold paint
medium paintbrush
stiff card (card stock)
pair of compasses (compass)
scissors
thick needle
wire cutters
fine brass wire
medium-sized transparent plastic crystal bead drops
round-nosed jewellery pliers
medium-sized transparent plastic crystal beads
large and small coloured beads

1 Paint the sconce gold to give a gilded effect. Leave to dry. You may need more than one coat to achieve good coverage.

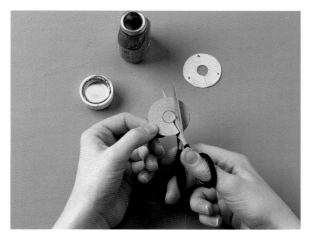

2 Cut two discs of stiff card (card stock). These will be inserted in the joints where the sconce arms unscrew to allow for wiring, so should be a little wider than the arms at this point. Paint the discs gold and leave to dry. Cut out the centres to fit around the wires. Make a cut from the edge to the centre of each so that it can be opened, then use a thick needle to punch three equidistant holes between the inner and outer edges.

3 Make up three bead drops for each disc. The links are made with individual lengths of wire to give flexibility. Using the wire cutters, cut a piece of wire about 3cm/1¼in long. Thread on the base crystal bead drop and use the pliers to twist the wire once. Leave the ends open.

▶

4 Take a second length of wire of about the same length and make a small closed loop at one end using the pliers. Slip this loop over one of the open ends of the previous wire and twist the open ends together to secure the link. Trim the excess wire.

5 Thread on a medium-sized transparent bead. Cut the wire to 8mm/⅜in and make another closed loop. Cut another length of wire, thread it through and make another closed loop. Thread on a small coloured bead. Repeat the looping process to add one more medium transparent bead. Add the final length of wire.

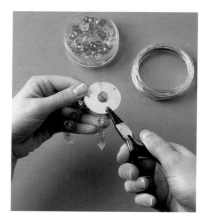

6 Repeat Steps 3–5 for the remaining drops. Attach the drops to the gold-painted discs, looping the wires through the punched holes.

7 Decide where the swags will be positioned on the sconce and measure the swagged length between the two points. Make up the swags using the same looped wire method as before, alternating a medium transparent bead with a small coloured bead. At the centre of the swag, place a large coloured bead as a focal point.

8 Attach the swags by wrapping the ends of the wire around the arms of the sconce at least twice and twisting. Fit the gold discs in the joints of the sconce arms.

TRINKET BOX

This delicate mosaic is made entirely from old cups and plates. Plain white pieces are used for the
borders around the squares, which contain individual flowers made of patterned china.

YOU WILL NEED
wooden box
PVA (white) glue
mixing bowl
old household paintbrush
bradawl or other sharp instrument
soft dark pencil
tile nippers
protective goggles
old china: white and patterned
cement-based tile adhesive
admix
flexible (putty) knife
rubber (latex) gloves
cloth or sponge
paint scraper
soft cloth, for polishing

1 Prime the top and sides of
the wooden box with diluted
PVA (white) glue. Leave to dry,
then score at random with a
bradawl or other sharp implement.

2 Using a soft pencil, and the
template at the back of the
book, draw a grid on the box.
Draw a flower in each square,
with a large flower in the centre.

3 Using tile nippers and wearing goggles, cut white
pieces of china into small squares. Mix the tile
adhesive with admix. Using a flexible (putty) knife,
spread this along the grid lines, a small area at a time.

4 Press the white tesserae into the adhesive in neat,
close-fitting rows. Cover all the grid lines on the
top and sides of the box. Leave to dry overnight.

▶

5 Wearing goggles and using tile nippers, cut out small patterned pieces from the china. Sort them into colours. Position the tesserae on the box and plan out the colour scheme.

6 Wearing rubber (latex) gloves, spread the tile adhesive and admix over each square of the top and sides in turn. Press in the tesserae (tiles) to make each flower and the background. Leave to dry.

7 Still wearing rubber gloves, spread tile adhesive all over the surface of the mosaic, getting right into the crevices. Wipe off any excess adhesive with a damp cloth or sponge.

8 Using a flexible (putty) knife, smooth the tile adhesive around the hinges and clasp, if there is one. Remove any excess adhesive immediately with a cloth before it dries. Leave to dry.

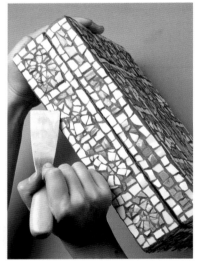

9 Carefully scrape off any tile adhesive, which may have dried on the surface of the mosaic, with a paint scraper. Take care not to scratch the surface of the tesserae.

10 When all the excess grout has been removed, polish the surface of the box with a soft cloth, rubbing each china fragment to a high shine.

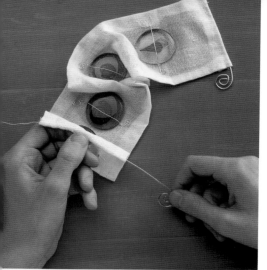

bathrooms

Bathrooms have come of decorating age, and deservedly so. But creating a bathroom that you actually want to spend time in requires a little more ingenuity than simply stacking colour co-ordinated towels and arranging empty perfume bottles. The inspirational ideas in this section will help you design a bathroom in which you can wash, shower, bathe and, perhaps most importantly of all, unwind.

Creams, whites and pastels are always popular in the bathroom – they make a small room look larger – but there's no need to adhere strictly to pale colours. Why not evoke memories of childhood holidays by adorning the walls with a vibrant sandcastle frieze or make a bathroom cabinet in dazzling Caribbean colours? For a really dramatic effect, treat your bathroom floor to a mosaic makeover and cover it with a wonderful tiled design with a sea-faring motif. The view from the bath is looking better all the time! Above all, bathrooms need to be practical, so consider adorning the walls with tile splashbacks to create a backdrop that is both waterproof and easy to wipe clean.

What about views you don't want to see? Cover over windows with a woven organza blind, which does not reduce light levels, or hide away unsightly objects in a papier-mâché wall store (cabinet). Using stained glass techniques in the bathroom to treat mirrors and windows creates a look that is fresh and eye-catching. Just remember that these are all simple solutions that can be achieved in a weekend.

SANDCASTLE FRIEZE

Evocative of childhood summers spent on the beach, sandcastles are simple, colourful shapes to stencil. Perfect for a child's room or for a family bathroom, they will bring a touch of humour to your walls. Paint the flags in different colours or glue on paper flags for added interest.

YOU WILL NEED
emulsion (latex) paints in blue and white
paintbrush
household sponge
acetate
craft knife and cutting mat
tape measure
pencil
masking tape
stencil paints in yellow, black and other colours of your choice
stencil brushes
fine paintbrush
coloured paper (optional)
PVA (white) glue (optional)

1 Paint below dado (chair) rail height in blue. When dry, rub on white emulsion (latex) with a sponge. Trace the templates at the back of the book. Cut the stencils from acetate (see Techniques).

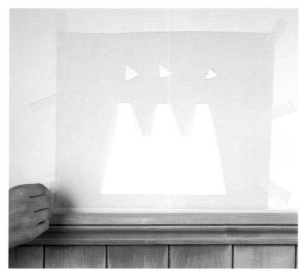

2 Measure the wall to calculate how many sand-castles you can fit on and make light pencil marks at regular intervals. Hold the stencil above the dado rail and secure the corners with masking tape.

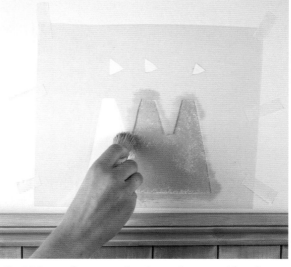

3 Using yellow stencil paint and a stencil brush, stencil in the first sandcastle.

150

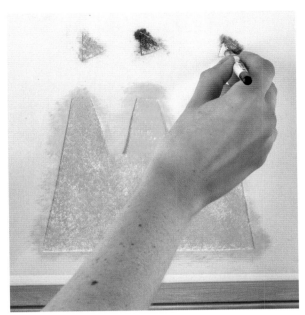

4 Stencil each flag in a different colour and remove the stencil.

5 When the paint has dried, stencil a star on the sandcastle in a contrasting colour of paint.

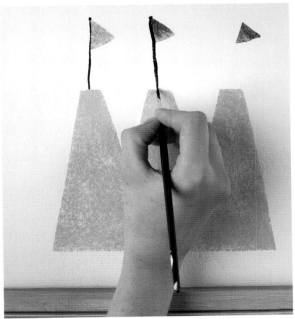

6 Using a fine paintbrush and black stencil paint, paint in the flagpoles.

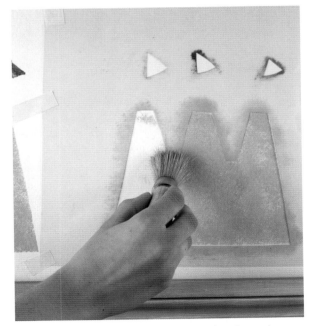

7 Continue stencilling the sandcastles along the wall using your pencil marks to position them. ▶

8 As an alternative to stencilling the flags, cut out triangles of coloured paper and glue them to the wall with PVA (white) glue, then paint in the flagpoles.

Above: Don't be too exacting when painting the flagpoles. Wobbly lines and erratic angles add to the child-like quality of the sandcastle frieze.

Left: A variation on the seashore theme might include bright tropical shapes in Caribbean colours.

WOVEN ORGANZA BLIND

Glamorous metallic organza lets the daylight through while obscuring the view from outside, so this sparkling woven blind, with its delicate, watery sheen, would be particularly appropriate for an unfrosted bathroom window.

YOU WILL NEED
scissors
metallic organza in two different colours
tape measure
pins
tacking (basting) thread
needle
sewing machine
matching thread
9mm/³⁄₈in wooden dowel to fit across the window
2 screw-in hooks

1 Cut the metallic organza into strips 5cm/2in wide, at right angles to the selvedge. The vertical strips, in one colour, should be at least 10cm/4in longer than the finished blind length, and the horizontal strips in the other colour should be about 4cm/1½in wider than the finished width. Fray the edges of all the strips.

2 On a large table, lay out the horizontal strips of organza.

3 Interweave the vertical and horizontal strips, pinning each intersection.

4 Leave 7.5cm/3in tabs along the top edge. When the required size has been reached, tack (baste) all round the outside edge.

155

5 Fold over the tabs along the top edge and tack (baste) in place.

6 Machine-stitch right around the edge of the woven area.

7 Trim the sides and lower edge of the woven area back to 2.5cm/1in.

8 Thread the wooden dowel through the loops along the top. Screw two hooks into the top corners of the window frame to hang the blind.

BLACK-AND-WHITE FLOOR

No artistic skills are required for this stunning mosaic, as the picture is simply an old etching enlarged on a photocopier. The tesserae (tiles) are glued on to fibreglass mesh, then lowered into position on the floor.

YOU WILL NEED
black-and-white image
clear plastic film (wrap)
masking tape
fibreglass mesh
tile nippers
protective goggles
unglazed mosaic ceramic tiles: black and white
PVA (white) glue
mixing bowl
fine artist's paintbrush, for glue
craft knife
cement-based tile adhesive
rubber (latex) gloves
notched spreader
flat wooden board
hammer
soft cloth

1 Decide on the image you wish to use: you may wish to build up a picture from various elements. Enlarge on a photocopier to the required size.

2 Working on a large work surface, cover the photocopy with clear plastic film (wrap) and secure the edges with masking tape. If your picture is built up of more than one image, repeat this process for all sections. ▶

157

3 Position a piece of fibreglass mesh over the plastic film (wrap) and tape down to the work surface with masking tape. Using tile nippers and wearing goggles, cut the tiles into quarters.

4 Beginning with the main features such as this boat, glue the tesserae (tiles) to the fibreglass mesh using a fine paintbrush. Build up the picture, using the light and shade of the photocopy as a guide.

5 Outline the panel with a geometric border in black and white, cutting some of the tesserae in half to make triangular shapes.

6 Fill in the background of the design, simplifying and accentuating the black and white areas, until the photocopy is completely covered. Leave to dry.

7 Using a craft knife, cut through the mesh and plastic, chopping the mosaic into manageable sections. You may find it helpful to cut around the boat shape as shown.

8 Turn the sections over and peel off the plastic. Using the craft knife, pierce any holes in the mesh that are clogged with glue.

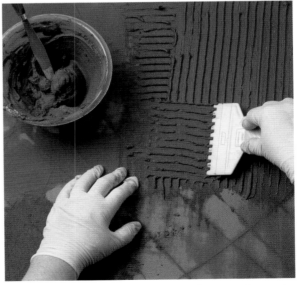

9 Mix the adhesive according to the manufacturer's instructions. Wearing rubber (latex) gloves, spread over the bathroom floor, using a notched spreader. ▶

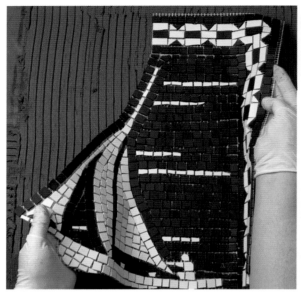

10 Carefully lay each section of the mosaic on the tile adhesive, mesh side down.

11 Place a flat board over each part of the mosaic and tap with a hammer to make sure the tesserae (tiles) are firmly embedded into the adhesive. Leave to dry overnight, then grout with more tile adhesive (see Techniques). Polish with a soft cloth.

SPLASHBACK SQUARES

Mosaic is an ideal surface for decorating bathrooms and kitchens since it is waterproof and easy to wipe clean. This simple design is made of tiles in two colours, alternated to give a checkerboard effect. Choose the colours to match your bathroom fittings.

YOU WILL NEED

12mm/½in thick plywood, cut to fit along the top of your basin
or sink and half as deep
PVA (white) glue
mixing bowl
old household paintbrush
bradawl or other sharp implement
soft dark pencil
tile nippers
protective goggles
thin glazed ceramic household tiles, in 2 contrasting colours
flexible (putty) knife
rubber (latex) gloves
white cement-based tile adhesive
notched spreader or cloth pad
sandpaper
yacht varnish
screwdriver
4 domed mirror screws

1 Prime both sides of the plywood with diluted PVA (white) glue. Leave to dry, then score one side with a sharp implement.

2 Divide the scored side of the plywood into eight squares. Draw a motif into each square using the templates at the back of the book.

3 Make a hole in each corner of the plywood, using a bradawl. These will form the holes for the screws to fix the splashback to the wall.

163

4 Using tile nippers, and wearing goggles to protect your eyes, cut the tiles into random shapes. Here the motifs are picked out alternately in dark blue and pale yellow, with the other colour used as the background. Following your drawn designs, stick the tiles in place with PVA (white) glue over the pencil markings on each square. Position the tiles carefully around the holes made for hanging. When each square is glued into position, wipe off any excess glue with a soft pad, before it dries. Leave until completely dry, preferably overnight.

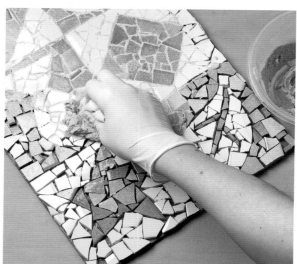

5 Wearing rubber (latex) gloves, mix the tile adhesive as recommended by the manufacturer. Wipe it over the surface of the mosaic with a notched spreader or cloth pad, smoothing around the edges with your fingers. Wipe off any excess adhesive and re-open the screw holes. Leave to dry overnight.

6 Carefully sand off any remaining dried adhesive on the surface of the mosaic. Paint the back of the plywood with yacht varnish to seal it and make it waterproof, and leave to dry for 1-2 hours. Fasten the splashback to the wall with mirror screws inserted through the four holes at each corner.

ON THE TILES

Small mosaic tiles make an attractive Mediterranean-style frame that would be perfect in a conservatory or bathroom. Plan the dimensions of the frame to suit the size of tiles, to avoid having to cut and fit odd-shaped pieces.

YOU WILL NEED
pencil and metal ruler
2cm/¾in thick medium-density fibreboard (MDF)
saw
drill and jigsaw
wood glue
white acrylic primer
paintbrush
tile cement
notched spreader
glass mosaic tiles
rubber (latex) gloves
grout
soft cloth
mirror
narrow picture moulding
2 ring screws
brass picture wire

1 Draw a frame on medium–density fibreboard (MDF). Cut out using a saw. Drill corner holes for the centre and cut out with a jigsaw. Cut out a shelf and glue to the frame with wood glue. Let dry.

2 Prime both sides of the frame and shelf with white acrylic primer to seal it.

3 Apply tile cement to a small area, using a finely notched spreader. ▶

165

4 Apply a random selection of tiles, leaving a 2mm/¹⁄₁₆in gap between each tile. Continue over the rest of the frame, working on a small area at a time. Tile the edges with a single row of tiles.

5 Following the manufacturer's instructions, let the tile cement dry for a couple of hours. Next, wearing rubber (latex) gloves, spread grout in between the tiles, scraping off the excess.

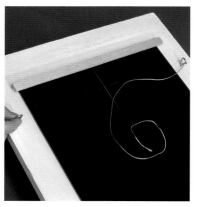

6 Clean off any remaining grout with a soft cloth. Let the grout dry thoroughly.

7 Lay a mirror face down on the back of the frame and secure it with narrow picture moulding, glued in place with wood glue. Let dry.

8 Finally, screw two ring screws in place on the back of the mirror, and tie on picture wire to hang the frame.

NAUTICAL WALL-STORE

This jaunty wall-hanging provides safe storage for all those important little odds and ends
that are always going astray. Hung in the bathroom, it makes the ideal place to keep
nail varnish (polish) and cotton wool balls.

YOU WILL NEED
balloon
newspaper
wallpaper paste
mixing bowl
scissors
heavy corrugated cardboard
marker pen
ruler
PVA (white) glue
medium and fine paintbrushes
masking tape
fine sandpaper
white (emulsion) paint
picture-hanging eyelet
acrylic paints
paint-mixing container
acrylic spray varnish

1 Blow up the balloon fully to make a firm base for
the papier-mâché. Tear newspaper into 2.5cm/
1in strips and soak in wallpaper paste. Cover the lower
two-thirds of the balloon in five layers of
papier-mâché.

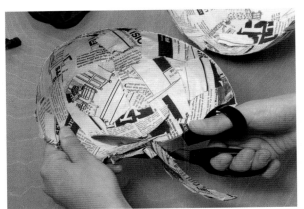

2 Leave the papier-mâché in a warm place until
completely dry. Burst the balloon and remove it.
Using scissors, trim the top of the bowl evenly, then
cut it in half.

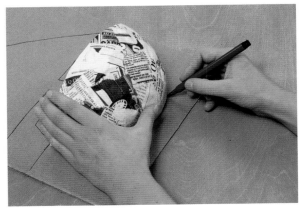

3 On a sheet of heavy corrugated cardboard, draw
the mast, sails and cabin of the boat. Place the
half-bowl in position and draw around it to complete
the boat.

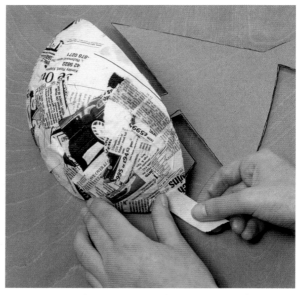

4 Cut the boat shape out of the cardboard using strong scissors. Seal the cardboard with a coat of diluted PVA (white) glue and leave to dry.

5 Using masking tape, attach the papier-mâché bowl section to the cardboard shape.

6 Cover the sails and the back of the boat with layers of papier-mâché and add another layer to the bowl. Leave in a warm place to dry completely.

7 Rub down lightly with fine sandpaper, then prime with two coats of white emulsion (latex). Allow to dry. Attach an eyelet to the top of the mast. Decorate using acrylic paints and spray with varnish.

FISH MOSAIC SPLASHBACK

Beads clustered together make an original addition to mosaics, and are perfect for creating intricate shapes. Use a mixture of sizes and colours for the fish, and stick to one type of bead for the starfish for a contrasting effect.

YOU WILL NEED
pencil
paper
piece of plywood to fit splashback area
carbon paper
glass mosaic tiles in a variety of colours
wood glue
interior filler
mixing container
spoon
acrylic paints in a variety of colours
selection of beads including metallic bugle beads, frosted and metallic square beads, large round beads and mixed beads
mosaic clippers
tile grout
cloth

1 Sketch the design to fit the splashback on a large sheet of paper, keeping the shapes simple and bold. Use a sheet of carbon paper to transfer the design to the plywood by drawing firmly over all the lines using a pencil.

2 Apply the mosaic border. Lay out all the tiles first, alternating the colours. Then apply wood glue to the border, a small section at a time, positioning the tiles as you go.

3 Following the manufacturer's instructions, mix up a small amount of interior filler, then add some acrylic paint to colour it to match the beads.

4 Spread green filler thickly over the seaweed fronds, then carefully press in metallic green bugle beads.

5 Fill in the fish fins using green filler and metallic green square beads. Make sure all the beads are on their sides so that the holes don't show. Spread orange filler thickly over the starfish and press in square frosted beads. Use some darker beads for shading.

6 Glue on a large bead for the fish eye using wood glue. Thickly spread white filler onto a 5cm/2in square section of the fish body and press in mixed beads. Repeat, working in small sections, until the fish is complete. Glue on large beads for bubbles.

7 For the background and rocks, use mosaic clippers to cut the mosaic tiles into 1cm/½in squares.

8 Stick the tiles in place with wood glue, varying the shades. Clip the edges of the tiles to fit around curved areas of the design. Mix up tile grout following the manufacturer's instructions and, wearing rubber (latex) gloves, spread over the completed design. Spread very lightly and carefully over the beaded areas. Wipe off the grout with a damp cloth and leave to dry.

SEASHORE BATHROOM SET

Imaginative designs applied to a plain soapdish and toothbrush holder will transform the look of your bathroom. Use this delightful watery motif with any combination of colours.

YOU WILL NEED

plain china soapdish and toothbrush holder or mug
cleaning fluid & cloth
tracing paper
soft pencil
plain paper
adhesive spray
carbon paper
scalpel or scissors
clear adhesive tape
felt-tipped pen
water-based ceramic paints: mid blue, ivory, turquoise, lemon, pink and dark blue
medium and fine artist's paintbrushes
paint palette

1 Thoroughly clean the china, using cleaning fluid and a cloth, to remove all traces of dust and dirt.

2 Trace the templates at the back of the book and enlarge if necessary. Transfer the designs on to a piece of plain paper. Spray the back of the paper with glue and stick on to a sheet of carbon paper, carbon side down. Cut out the designs, leaving a margin all round. Tape the designs on to the china pieces. Transfer the outlines lightly with a felt-tipped pen and remove the carbon paper designs.

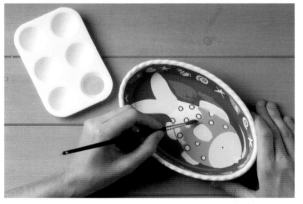

3 Using a medium paintbrush, paint in the blue background colour on the soapdish and tooth-brush holder. When completely dry, paint in the fish and shells on the soapdish.

▶

4 Paint the fish and shells on the toothbrush holder in the same way as for the soapdish, using a medium paintbrush. Allow the paint to dry.

5 Using a fine paintbrush and dark blue paint, sketch in detailing for the fish and shells.

6 Add the border to the soap dish and the final touches to the toothbrush holder. Paint white dots and squiggles, to create a watery feel. Let dry.

PAINTED DRAWERS

Jazz up plain, unfinished drawers with bright paintbox colours and simple daisy stencils. The same stencils could be used to decorate larger pieces of furniture such as a chest of drawers for a child's room or to update plain kitchen units. Emulsion (latex) sample pots are ideal to use on small projects.

YOU WILL NEED
set of wooden drawers
sandpaper
emulsion (latex) paints in various colours
paintbrush
screwdriver
acetate
craft knife and cutting mat
stencil brush
matt (flat) acrylic varnish
wood glue (optional)

1 Remove the drawers and sand down the frame and drawers to remove any rough areas or patches of old paint.

2 Paint the drawer frame using emulsion (latex) paint and a paintbrush. Leave to dry, then apply a second coat of paint.

3 Unscrew the drawer knobs and paint each drawer in a different-coloured emulsion paint. Leave to dry and apply a second coat. Trace the flower template at the back of the book and cut a stencil from acetate (see Techniques).

4 When the drawers are dry, position the flower stencil in the centre of a drawer and, using a stencil brush and paint in a contrasting colour, stencil on the flower. Leave to dry.

5 Stencil a flower in the centre of each drawer, using a different colour for each one.

6 Paint the drawer knobs with two coats of paint, leaving them to dry between coats. Leave to dry.

7 Screw or glue a painted knob to the centre of each drawer. Varnish the drawers with matt (flat) acrylic varnish. Leave to dry before reassembling.

ETCHED BATHROOM MIRROR

Mirror tiles make inexpensive canvases for practising your stained glass techniques. This one is decorated using etching paste and coloured stained glass cut into petals and randomly arranged into pretty flowers.

YOU WILL NEED

mirror tile

felt-tipped pen

ruler

glass cutter

rubber (latex) gloves

etching paste

paintbrush

clean cotton cloth

4mm/³⁄₁₆in copper foil

fid

flux (card)

soldering iron and solder

brass hanging wire

pieces of stained glass

epoxy glue

1 Mark up the size of your mirror using a felt-tipped pen on the surface of the mirror tile.

2 Cut out the mirror with a glass cutter.

3 Wearing rubber (latex) gloves and using the etching paste, paint ten or eleven four-petalled flowers around the edges of the mirror.

4 Wash off the etching paste after 3 minutes, and wipe the glass clean with a clean cotton cloth.

5 Wrap copper foil around the edge of the mirror and press down with a fid.

6 Solder around the copper foil. The heat will turn the copper foil a silver colour.

7 Cut a length of hanging wire and solder it to the edge of the mirror on each side.

8 Cut out small petal shapes in different coloured glass and stick them in flower shapes randomly around the edges of the mirror. Let the glue dry hard, and then clean the mirror with a clean cotton cloth.

GLASS NUGGET WINDOW HANGING

This window hanging is an easy project that is ideal for beginners. The simple materials of muslin fabric, coloured glass and silver wire complement each other perfectly and create a pleasingly fresh, uncluttered decoration.

YOU WILL NEED
50cm/20in white muslin
sharp scissors
white sewing thread
needle
copyright-free pictures of shells
(see templates)
acetate
epoxy glue
four large glass nuggets
fine silver jewellery wire
jewellery pliers
thick copper wire

1 Sketch your design to scale on a piece of paper. Draw the shape of the background on to the muslin, leaving extra to turn and edge the sides. Cut out the shape.

2 Sew a single hem around all the sides of the muslin rectangle.

3 Photocopy shell pictures on to acetate. Cut out the images using sharp scissors. ▶

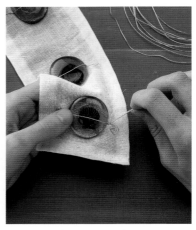

4 Glue the acetate shapes on to the muslin, spacing them equally down the muslin. Then glue the glass nuggets over the images. Make sure they do not stick to your worktop as the glue may seep through the material.

5 Cut pieces of silver wire long enough to fit across each glass nugget, leaving a little extra at either side. Curl each end into a spiral using the jewellery pliers.

6 Sew the pieces of wire securely to the muslin at each side of the glass nuggets.

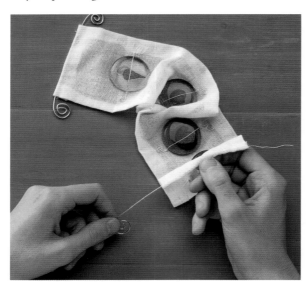

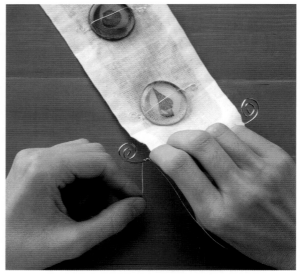

7 Take the copper wire, curl one end into a spiral using the small pliers, and slide the metal through the top hem of the material. Do the same on the bottom. Curl the other ends of both pieces of the wire when they are through.

8 Take some silver wire and wind it round the copper wire at the top end, on both sides of the material, for the piece to hang in the window.

halls
and studies

The hall gives the first hint of the style of decoration in a house and, if decorated correctly, can hint tantalizingly at what lies beyond. Treat the hall as a gloomy corridor between "more important" rooms, and this will be to the detriment of the whole house. Transforming these areas does not mean throwing everything out and starting from scratch. Give walls, furniture and surfaces a welcome makeover using imaginative crafts such as decoupage, mosaic-work and stained glass.

If you favour making a bold entrance, why not opt for the flamboyance of a Tuscan-style wall, using the simple technique of stamping, or deck out a table in a blaze of daisies, using mosaics? Create a charming door panel made from paper and card using the technique of decoupage or bring a degree of gravitas to the hallway by creating leaded panels for old doors.

Studies are often dismissed as utility rooms and tend to suffer stylistically as a result. If your budget is tight, this is usually the room that bears the brunt of economizing. But cost needn't be a restraint when breathing new life into your study. Bring the seasons into your study by embellishing a window with a design of falling leaves or uplift the room with an ornate stained-glass sunlight catcher. Any budding writers in the household would benefit from a decoupage waste bin to catch those creative out-takes. Who would believe that these simple changes could make such a dramatic difference?

TROMPE L'OEIL TUSCAN WALL

For a really dramatic effect, create an imitation Tuscan doorway on your wall. Paint on warm yellow, terracotta and green, and then sand back the paint to give the beautiful mellow appearance that normally only results from centuries of wear.

YOU WILL NEED

cream, warm yellow, terracotta and green
emulsion (latex) paint
small, large and medium paintbrushes
scrap paper
paint roller and tray
pencil
set square (T square)
spirit (carpenter's) level and straightedge
string
masking tape
artist's paintbrush
hand sander
brown pencil

1 Experiment with mixing the colours. You can use quite strong shades as they will soften when they are sanded back.

2 Using a paint roller, paint the wall surface with a base coat of cream emulsion (latex).

3 Wash over the base colour with warm yellow emulsion, using a large paintbrush.

4 Draw your design to scale on paper, using a set square (T square).

5 Draw the straight lines of the doorway and border design on the wall, using a level and straightedge.

188

6 Draw the upper curve of the doorway, using a pencil tied to a piece of string as shown.

7 Mask off the areas of the design that will be painted terracotta with masking tape.

8 Paint these areas with the terracotta emulsion, then remove the masking tape. Any smudging can be wiped off immediately.

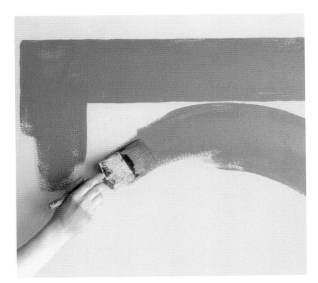

9 Using the medium paintbrush, paint the green area of the doorway. Use masking tape, if necessary, to mask off each area.

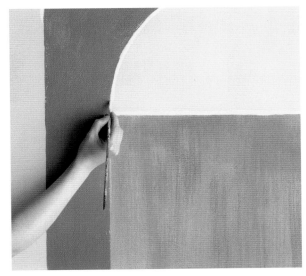

10 Using an artist's paintbrush, carefully paint a thin yellow outline around all the edges of the doorway. Leave to dry.

11 Lightly sand over the design, using a hand sander. Go back to the base coat in some areas and leave others untouched.

12 Wash over the design again with warm yellow emulsion (latex).

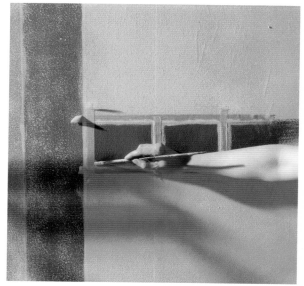

13 Mask off the squares in the border area with masking tape. Using an artist's paintbrush, outline each square in yellow and then immediately remove the masking tape.

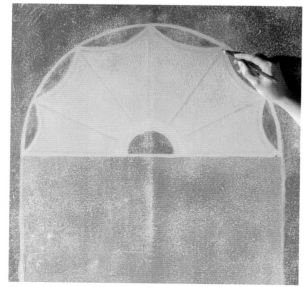

14 Using a brown pencil, draw in fine lines in the semicircular "fanlight" ("transom") as shown.

DAISY-COVERED CONSOLE

This wonderful table is literally strewn with daisies — green stems twine around the legs and a carpet of pretty white flowers spreads over the top. If the table has a rim, saw it off first to make the shape easier to mosaic.

YOU WILL NEED
small table
sandpaper
PVA (white) glue
mixing bowl
old household paintbrush
bradawl or other sharp implement
soft dark pencil
tile nippers
protective goggles
thin glazed ceramic household tiles: white,
yellow, green and pale pink
rubber (latex) gloves
cement-based tile adhesive
admix
flexible (putty) knife
hammer
heavy protective gloves
piece of sacking (heavy cloth)
notched spreader
sponge
dust mask
soft cloth

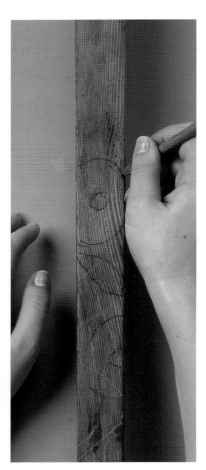

1 Remove any old wax, dirt, paint or varnish from the table, then sand and prime with diluted PVA (white) glue. Leave to dry, then score all the surfaces with a sharp implement.

2 Draw flowers and stems twisting around the legs and spreading over the tabletop, using the template at the back of the book, if desired. Take care when joining the legs to the tabletop.

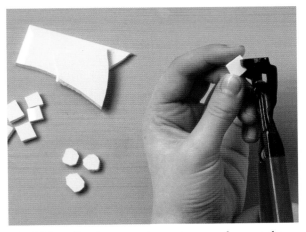

3 Using tile nippers and wearing goggles, cut the yellow tiles into small squares, then nip off the corners to make circles for the centres of the flowers.

4 Cut the white tiles into small, equally sized oblongs. Make these into petal shapes by nipping off the corners of each oblong.

5 Wearing rubber (latex) gloves, mix the tile adhesive and admix together. Using a flexible (putty) knife, spread over a pencilled flower outline. Press in a flower centre and petals — you may need to cut some petals on the legs in half. Complete all the flowers.

6 Spread a thin coat of the adhesive and admix mixture along the pencil outlines of the stems and leaves. Cut the green tiles into appropriate stem and leaf shapes and press in place. Leave to dry overnight.

▶

7 Using a hammer, and wearing goggles and heavy gloves for protection, break up the pink tiles. It is advisable to wrap each tile in a piece of sacking (heavy cloth) to prevent splintering and shattering.

8 Wearing rubber (latex) gloves and working on a small area at a time, spread tile adhesive and admix over the background areas. Press in the pink tile pieces to fit. Leave to dry overnight.

9 Wearing rubber gloves, grout the mosaic with tile adhesive. Use a notched spreader for the large flat areas. Wipe off the excess with a damp sponge and leave to dry overnight.

10 Wearing a dust mask, carefully sand the surface of the table to remove any lumps of dried adhesive still remaining. Wipe the table with a damp sponge if necessary, and polish with a soft cloth.

ON DISPLAY

A deep-sided, sectioned frame is the perfect way to display a collection of small objects such as ornaments, jewellery or badges. First plan the frame on paper so you can custom build the sections to suit the size of your collection.

YOU WILL NEED
pencil & metal ruler
length of 35 x 5mm/1¼ x ¼in batten
junior hacksaw
wood glue
panel pins (brads)
hammer
hardboard
white acrylic primer
paintbrush
length of 35 x 2mm/1¼ x ¹⁄₁₆in batten
masking tape
PVA (white) glue
tissue paper in assorted colours
acrylic paint in yellow, dark blue and light blue
Indian shisha mirrors

1 Make a rectangular frame with the thicker battening by gluing it with wood glue and securing it using panel pins (brads).

2 Glue and pin a piece of hardboard to the back. Coat the smooth front side with acrylic primer.

3 Measure and draw out the size of the compartments. Using the thinner battening, cut them out with a junior hacksaw.

4 Put the compartments together with wood glue, taping them with masking tape until they are dry.

5 Coat the wood with PVA (white) glue and cover with torn pieces of coloured tissue paper.

6 Work the tissue paper into the corners and keep applying the glue as necessary. Use lighter colours over stronger colours to create depth of colour.

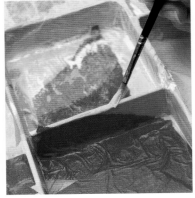

7 Touch up any areas that need more colour with the yellow acrylic paint.

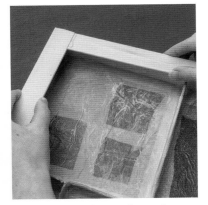

8 Glue the thinner battening to the outer edge of the frame, using wood glue.

9 Cover the edge of the frame with a collage of tissue paper glued on with PVA (white) glue.

10 Using a paintbrush, lightly brush over the tissue paper with blue acrylic paint.

11 Glue on small Indian shisha mirrors all around the frame edge.

12 Arrange your collection in the compartments, securing the pieces with glue or a re-usable adhesive, as preferred.

LEADED DOOR PANELS

The etched glass panels on this old door have been painted with glass paints and finished with stick-on lead. The finished effect has a much lighter look than genuine stained glass made with lead came.

YOU WILL NEED
door with two sandblasted glass panels
tape measure
paper and pencil
ruler
felt-tipped pen
scissors
masking tape
indelible black pen
self-adhesive lead 1cm/½in wide
craft knife and cutting mat
boning peg
glass paints in turquoise, green, yellow and light green
turpentine
small paintbrushes

1 Measure the glass panels with a tape measure. With a pencil, draw panels to scale on a piece of paper. Using a ruler, draw your design within the panel area, including 1cm/⅜in wide dividing lines to allow for the leading. Trace over the finished design in felt-tipped pen, cross hatching the lead lines.

2 Cut out this paper pattern with scissors and stick it to the reverse of one of the glass panels with lengths of masking tape.

3 Trace the design from the paper pattern on to the sandblasted side of the glass using an indelible black pen. When the tracing is complete, remove the paper pattern.

4 Stretch the lead by gently pulling it. Cut four lengths to fit around the edge of the glass panel, using a sharp craft knife. Remove the backing paper and stick the lead in place.

5 Measure the lead needed for the inner framework and cut with a knife using a side-to-side rocking motion. Keep the blade at a 90° angle to the lead to ensure a straight cut. Cut and stick longer lengths of lead first, then work the smaller pieces.

6 With the edges butted closely together, remove the backing paper from the lead and press into place with your fingertips. Then press firmly along the length of the lead with a boning peg to seal it to the glass. Press around the outer edges of the lead with the pointed end of the boning peg to achieve a neat, watertight finish.

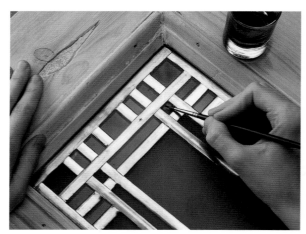

7 Dilute the glass paints with 30% turpentine to create a subtle, watercolour feel to the paint. Use a small paintbrush to colour in the small areas between the leading. Clean brushes with turpentine between colours.

8 Once the intricate areas are coloured in, paint the remainder of the design, leaving the centre of the glass panel unpainted or painting the whole area if you prefer. Leave to dry. Repeat for the other panel.

DOOR PLAQUE

It can be difficult to find door plaques, other than plain white, to suit contemporary homes. A clear glass plaque allows you to choose any design you like using motifs cut from greetings cards, wrapping paper or magazines. This quick project is ideal for beginners.

YOU WILL NEED
clear glass plaque
card (card stock)
craft knife
cutting mat
ruler
block of wood
masking tape
gold spray paint
pencil
magazine pictures and greetings cards
PVA (white) glue
clear water-based acrylic satin varnish
screwdriver and screws

1 Cut a rectangle of card (card stock) slightly bigger than the plaque, using a craft knife, cutting mat and ruler.

2 Tape the rectangle of card on to the wood.

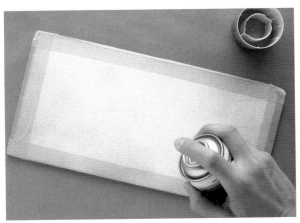

3 Spray with several thin coats of gold paint. Check the manufacturer's instructions — using with a primer gives a much bolder colour.

4 Draw a pencil line around the shape of the plaque in the centre of the card.

5 If using greetings cards, peel off the thick backing paper with a craft knife to make the paper thinner and easier to work with.

6 Dilute the PVA (white) glue half and half with water. Arrange the pictures into a pattern on the plaque-shaped panel and glue in place.

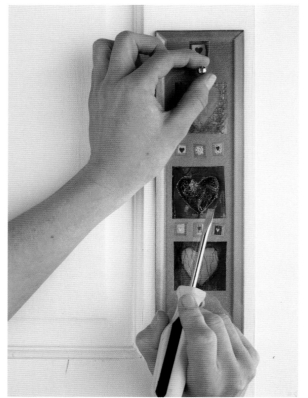

7 Cut out the panel around the pencil line using a craft knife and ruler. Coat with several layers of varnish, leaving to dry between coats.

8 Place the door plaque over the decorated panel and fix them both to the door, using screws and a screwdriver.

VALENTINE MIRROR

In this lovely hallway mirror, romantic red hearts and scrolling white lines are beautifully set off by the rich blue background, which sparkles with chunks of mirror glass. Choose the size and shape of the mirror to suit your wall space.

YOU WILL NEED

rectangle of 12mm/½in thick plywood, cut to size required
PVA (white) glue
mixing bowl
old household paintbrush
bradawl or other sharp implement
hand drill
mirror plate, with keyhole opening
screwdriver
12mm/½in screws
scissors
brown paper
masking tape
rectangle of mirror glass, cut to size required
ruler
soft dark pencil
cement-based tile adhesive
tile nippers
protective goggles
thin glazed ceramic household tiles: red, white and several
rich shades of blue
rubber (latex) gloves
hammer
heavy protective gloves
mirror glass tiles
piece of sacking (heavy cloth)
notched spreader
dust mask
fine sandpaper
soft cloth

1 Prime both sides of the plywood with diluted PVA (white) glue and leave to dry. Score one side (the front) with a sharp implement. Turn the board over and make a dent in the centre, using a drill. Screw the mirror plate over the dent.

2 Cut a piece of brown paper to the size of the mirror and tape it round the edge, to protect the glass. Mark its position in the centre front of the board and stick in place with tile adhesive.

3 Draw a small heart in the centre of each border and scrolling lines to connect the four hearts. Use the template at the back of the book if desired.

4 Using tile nippers and wearing goggles, cut the blue and red tiles into small, irregular pieces. Cut the white tiles into regular-sized squares.

5 Mix the tile adhesive as recommended by the manufacturer. Spread the adhesive over the pencilled heart shapes and press in the red tile pieces. Repeat for the white lines. Scrape off any excess adhesive and leave to dry overnight.

6 Using a hammer, and wearing goggles and rubber (latex) gloves to protect your eyes and hands, carefully break up the blue and mirror glass tiles into small pieces. It is advisable to wrap each tile in a piece of sacking (heavy cloth) before breaking it up, to avoid the tile shattering or splintering.

7 Working on a small area at a time, and wearing rubber (latex) gloves, spread tile adhesive over the background areas then press in the blue and glass pieces. Leave to dry overnight.

8 Grout the mosaic with tile adhesive, wearing rubber gloves as before. Use a notched spreader to distribute the glue over the flat surface and your gloved fingers for the edges.

9 Wearing a dust mask, carefully sand off any lumps of remaining adhesive that may have dried on the surface of the mosaic. Polish with a soft cloth.

10 For a professional finish, rub tile adhesive into the back of the plywood board. Remove the protective brown paper from the mirror.

SCREEN TEST

This screen is decorated with colour photocopies of flowers and leaves, and the scope for different colours and shapes is enormous. The combination of delicate gold tissue paper with pretty dried and photocopied flowers is very arresting.

YOU WILL NEED
unpainted screen
parchment-coloured matt emulsion (flat latex) paint
medium paintbrushes
pencil
tape measure
ruler
tissue paper
gold spray paint
wallpaper paste or PVA (white) glue
scissors
fresh leaves and flowers
craft knife
cutting mat
dried flowers and leaves
stencil card (card stock)
handmade paper
clear oil- or water-based satin varnish

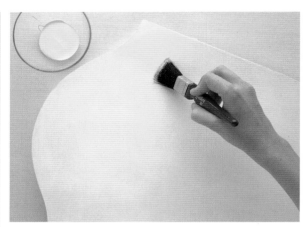

1 Paint the screen with one coat of parchment-coloured matt emulsion (flat latex) paint, using a medium paintbrush. Leave to dry completely, then apply a second coat of paint.

2 The screen is decorated with squares of tissue paper, so mark vertical and horizontal guidelines over the screen using a pencil, tape measure and ruler.

3 Spray the sheets of tissue paper with gold paint. Stick down squares of tissue on to the screen using a paintbrush and wallpaper paste or glue.

4 Cut pieces of tissue paper to fit the curved top edge of the screen and glue in place. Make colour photocopies of real leaves and flowers. Carefully cut out the shapes using a craft knife and cutting mat.

5 Select some dried flowers and leaves to decorate the curved top panels of the screen.

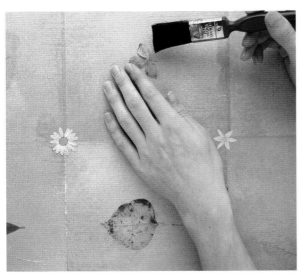

6 Arrange the leaf and flower photocopies on the screen and glue in position.

7 Arrange the dried flowers and leaves on the curved top sections and glue in place.

8 Make a tooth-edged pattern template out of
stencil card (card stock). Use this to cut out strips
of edging from handmade paper.

9 Glue the strips to the edges of the screen. When
the glue is dry, cover the screen with two coats
of satin varnish, leaving to dry between coats.

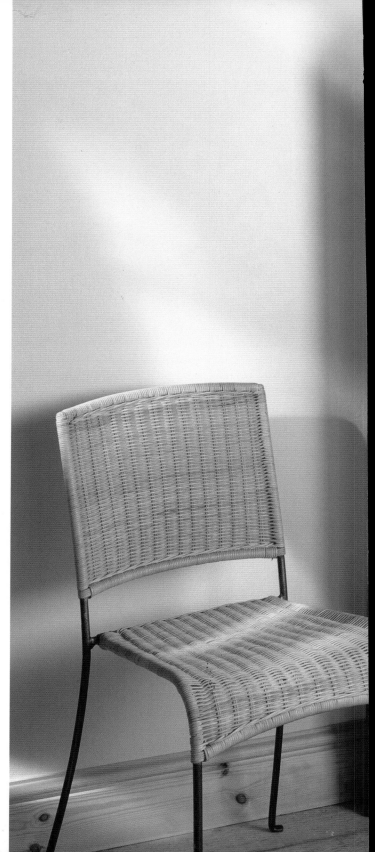

LEAFY WINDOW

The autumn leaves tumbling down this translucent panel look as if they are falling from the trees outside. These are cut out of paper, but if you find some beautiful real leaves you could press them and put them in the pockets instead.

YOU WILL NEED
scissors
organza
tape measure
iron
pins
matching thread
sewing machine
tracing paper
pencil
coloured paper in several autumnal shades
small scissors
wooden batten to fit across window
staple gun

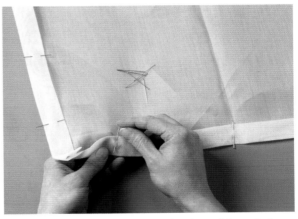

1 Cut a piece of organza to the size of the window plus 5cm/2in for hems all round. Turn in, press and pin 2.5cm/1in double hems down both sides and across the lower edge.

2 Use matching thread and a machine satin stitch to stitch over the fold of each hem.

3 Decide how many leaves you will have room for on your panel. Copy the leaf templates at the back of the book and trace on to coloured paper.

215

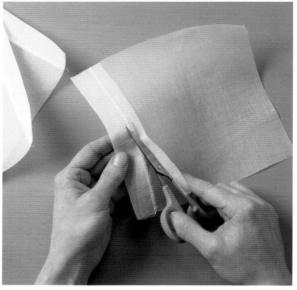

4 Cut out the paper leaves with a pair of small scissors.

5 Cut organza pockets to fit the leaf shapes, allowing an extra 2.5cm/1in at the upper edge. Fold over the hem allowance, press and satin-stitch 2cm/¾in from the edge. Trim off the excess fabric.

6 Pin and satin-stitch the pockets in place on the panel. Insert a leaf in each pocket, alternating the colours to make a pleasing design.

7 Lay the wooden batten along the top of the blind, pull the fabric tightly around the batten and staple in place at the back.

SUNLIGHT CATCHER

Stained glass is made for sunlight, and this sunlight catcher can hang in any window in the house to catch all of the available light. Gold outlining paste separates the coloured areas and adds an extra special shine.

YOU WILL NEED
20cm/8in diameter clear glass roundel, 4mm/³⁄₁₆in thick
4 mm/³⁄₁₆ in thick
paper and pencil
indelible black pen
gold outlining paste
glass paints in orange, yellow, red and blue
small paintbrushes
turpentine
73cm/29in length of chain
pliers
epoxy glue

1 Make a template by drawing around the rim of the glass roundel.

2 Trace the sun motif template from the back of the book, enlarging to the size required.

3 Place the circle of glass over the template and trace the design on to the glass using an indelible black pen.

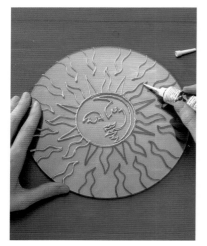

4 Trace over the black lines using gold outlining paste. Leave to dry.

5 Colour in the central sun motif using orange and yellow glass paints. Leave to dry. Clean brushes with turpentine.

6 Fill in the rest of the design using red and blue glass paints. Leave to dry. Clean brushes again.

7 Place the chain around the edge of the glass and cut to size. Rejoin the links by squeezing firmly together with pliers.

8 Cut an 8cm/3¼in length of chain, open the links at each end, and attach it to the chain circle by squeezing with pliers. Glue the chain circle around the circumference of the glass using epoxy glue.

PEBBLE WALL CLOCK

Natural materials on a papier-mâché base make an understated, stylish clock. A dozen sea-smoothed pebbles mark the hours: their subtle shades and polished surfaces contrast beautifully with the textures of grainy recycled paper and rough natural twine.

YOU WILL NEED
pencil
pair of compasses (compass)
ruler
heavy corrugated cardboard
craft knife
cutting mat
PVA (white) glue
newspaper
mixing bowl
paintbrush
fine sandpaper
white emulsion (latex) paint
decorative recycled paper
scissors
natural twine
clock movement and hands
strong, clear glue
12 pebbles
picture-hanging eyelet

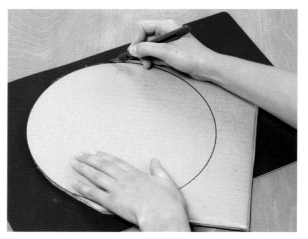

1 Draw a circle with a diameter of 25cm/10in on a piece of heavy corrugated cardboard. Cut it out using a craft knife and a cutting mat. Brush with diluted PVA (white) glue to seal it and leave it to dry.

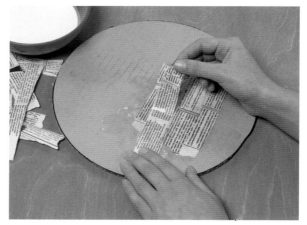

2 Tear newspaper into 2.5cm/1in wide strips, coat them with diluted PVA glue and cover the cardboard with five layers of papier-mâché.

3 Leave the clock in a warm place overnight. When it is completely dry, lightly smooth the surface of the clock using fine sandpaper.

4 Prime both sides of the clock with two coats of white emulsion (latex) paint, allowing the paint to dry between coats.

5 Draw a circle with a diameter of 18cm/7in on a sheet of decorative recycled paper, and cut it out. Use PVA glue to fix it in the centre of the clock face.

6 Apply a thick coat of PVA glue from the outer edge of the clock to the edge of the paper circle. Starting next to the paper, coil the twine around the clock face until the whole area is covered.

7 Using a sharp pencil, make a hole in the centre of the clock face for the spindle of the clock movement. Following the manufacturer's instructions, attach the movement and hands to the clock.

8 Turn the clock hands to 12 o'clock and make a mark on the twine border. Rotate the hands, marking the position of each hour on the dial.

9 Using strong, clear glue, attach a pebble at each mark on the twine to represent the hours. When the glue is thoroughly dry, attach a picture-hanging eyelet to the back of the clock.

DECOUPAGE WASTE BIN

Brown parcel wrap is used for the top layer of papier-mâché on this sturdy bin and makes the perfect background for the gold gift-wrap decoupage decorations. Vary the size and pattern of the decorations to give depth and an interesting texture to the bin.

YOU WILL NEED
pair of compasses (compass)
pencil
metal ruler
heavy corrugated cardboard
craft knife
cutting mat
gummed paper tape
sponge
PVA (white) glue
paintbrush
paper
wallpaper paste
mixing bowl
brown parcel wrap
gift-wrap
acrylic spray varnish

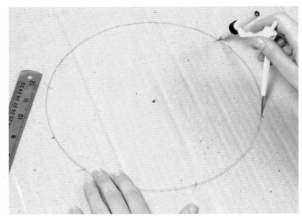

1 Using a pair of compasses (compass), draw a circle with a radius of 13cm/5in on heavy corrugated cardboard (card stock). Divide the circumference into 6 sections using the compasses.

2 Reduce the radius of the compasses to 6.5cm/ 2½in and mark off six intersecting arcs, so that the circle is divided into 12. Join the marks to give a 12-sided shape and cut out using the craft knife.

3 Cut out a sheet of corrugated cardboard 78 x 35cm/31 x 14in. (The corrugations should run vertically down the sides of the bin.) Divide it into 12 sections, 6.5cm/2½in wide, and rule a line 5cm/2in from the top edge. Score along all the lines.

4 Fold over the 5cm/2in strip across the top to make the border of the waste bin.

5 Cut 12 pieces of gummed paper tape and stick them to each edge of the bin base, moistening them with a damp sponge.

6 Turn the base over and use the tape to attach the sides to the base, bending the sides along the scored lines.

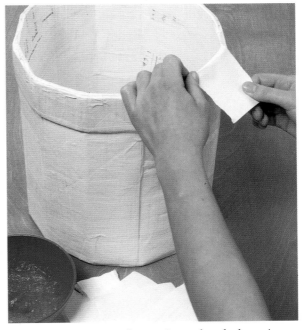

7 Use gummed paper tape to join the side seam, taking the tape over the top edge and down inside the bin. Seal the cardboard with a coat of diluted PVA (white) glue.

8 Tear some paper into strips and soak the strips in wallpaper paste. Apply four layers of papier-mâché to the bin, inside and out, and leave in a warm place to dry.

9 Apply a final layer of papier-mâché using brown parcel wrap. Allow to dry. To decorate the bin, tear images from a sheet of gift-wrap.

10 Paste the images with undiluted PVA (white) glue and arrange them all over the bin as you wish.

11 Tear some narrow strips of gift-wrap and stick these to the rim of the bin and the line below the raised border.

12 Protect the bin inside and out with a coat of acrylic spray varnish. Leave to dry.

LAMPSHADE TECHNIQUES

Making and decorating lampshades and bases is simple to do, and once you have mastered a few simple techniques you will be able to create a variety of exciting lamps.

MAKING BIAS BINDING (TAPE)
Bias binding strips may be used to wrap frames, cover raw edges or to bind edges decoratively.

1 Cut a rectangular piece of fabric on the straight grain. Fold down one top corner to meet the bottom edge, forming a diagonal fold. Press.

2 Open out the fabric. Mark parallel lines diagonally across the fabric 3cm/1¼in apart and cut out the strips.

GATHERING FABRIC

3 Pin the short edges together as shown and stitch the seam, using a sewing machine. Press the seam allowance open.

Thread a needle, double up the thread and tie a knot in the ends. Work an even running stitch the length of the fabric, draw up the thread, wind it around a pin and even out the gathers.

BINDING A FRAME USING BIAS BINDING OR
BINDING TAPE

Bind the frame to ensure a good surface for gluing a
fabric cover or to stitch fabric to a frame.

To start winding, turn 2.5cm/1in of the tape over a
strut and wind the tape along the strut at a 45° angle.
Secure the end with a few small stitches.

MEASURING A CONE-SHAPED FRAME

1 To find the circumference of the top and bottom
of a cone-shaped frame, measure the diameter
and multiply by three.

MAKING A PAPER PATTERN FOR A CONE-SHAPED OR
DRUM FRAME

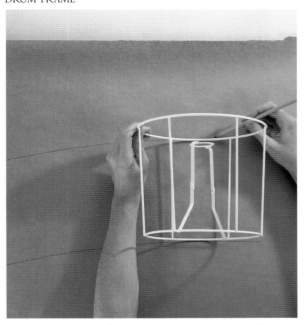

Place the frame at the end of a piece of paper. Draw
along one upright strut, then roll the frame across the
paper in an arc, marking the course of the outside top
and bottom rings until the first strut touches the paper
again. Add a 1cm/½in overlap allowance on one side.
Cut out and check it fits the frame.

2 To find the height of a cone-shaped frame,
measure the angled side of the frame, including
the struts.

MEASURING FOR A SHADE USING TWO RINGS

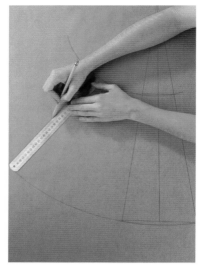

MAKING A LAMPSHADE USING
SELF-ADHESIVE BACKING MATERIAL
Lampshades can be simple to make
and homemade versions will fit
your own requirements perfectly.

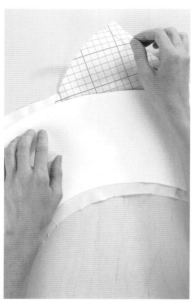

1 Measure the diameter of the
   top and bottom rings. In the
corner of a sheet of paper, parallel
to the bottom, mark the diameter
of the bottom ring. Draw a
vertical line at right angles,
bisecting the first line. Mark a
point along the vertical line the
desired height of the shade. At this
point draw a horizontal line the
length of the diameter of the top
ring. The mid-point should
intersect the vertical line. Draw a
diagonal line from the end of the
bottom line to the end of the top
line, and continue until it meets
the vertical line. Repeat on the
other side. Attach a pencil to a
piece of string, and place the
pencil on one of the points where
the top horizontal line meets the
diagonal. Pin the string at the
point where the vertical and
diagonal lines intersect. Draw an
arc. Repeat, using the bottom line.

2 Calculate the length of the
   circumference of the top ring
and mark this measurement on the
upper arc, starting from one of the
diagonal lines. Mark the length of
the circumference of the bottom
ring on the lower arc. Join these
two points. Add a 1 cm/½ in
overlap allowance to the side edge.

FLAME-PROOFING A LAMPSHADE
Fabric and paper must be rendered
flameproof. Before use, all shades
and decorations should be sprayed
with flame-retardant spray. Spray
in a well-ventilated area, wearing
a protective face mask if you suffer
from any respiratory problems.
Protective rubber (latex) gloves
are also advised. For application,
follow the manufacturer's
instructions. Always ensure that
both the shade and frame are dry
before attaching any wires or
exposing them to electricity.

1 Cut out the backing material
   to the size of the lampshade
template. For the lampshade cover,
lay the template on the fabric on
the cross. Draw around it, adding
a turning allowance of 1.5cm/
⅝in all round, and cut out.
Remove the backing paper from
the backing material and place it
sticky side down on the wrong
side of the fabric, leaving an even
turning allowance all round the
backing material. Smooth out the
fabric from the middle outwards.

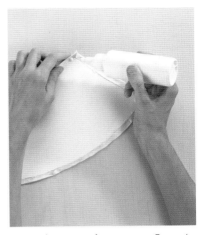

2 Clip away the corners 5mm/ ¼in from the corners of the backing material. Apply a line of glue around the turning allowance and fold it in half.

3 Apply another thin line of glue around the turning allowance, fold over all four corners, and then fold in the top and side edges.

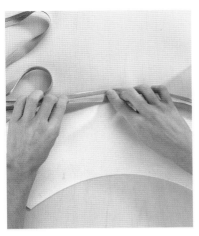

4 Apply a thin line of glue around the bottom edge. Press one side of the bias binding (tape) in position, all the way along the bottom edge.

5 Wrap the frame cover around the frame now or insert once the cover is glued and stitched. To wrap the frame, apply glue to the outside edges of the rings and struts and wrap the cover around the frame. Squeeze a line of glue along the inside of one side edge and lap (press) it over the opposite edge. Hold the edges firmly with two clothes pegs (pins) until dry.

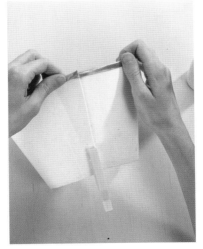

6 Where the ends of the bias binding meet, turn under 1cm/½in of one raw end and stick it down so that it overlaps the other raw end.

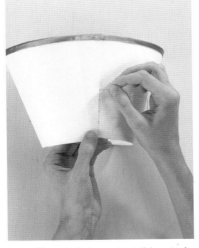

7 Slip stitch is an invisible stitch used to join folded edges and attach trimmings. With the needle, catch a thread under the fabric together with a thread on the fold of the fabric or trimming and make tiny, neat, evenly spaced stitches.

BEADWORK TECHNIQUES

Many of the techniques used in beadwork are quite straightforward. Work your way slowly through the instructions below to familiarize yourself with the methods.

SECURING BEADS

To fasten off (secure) a string or a single bead, pass the needle under the main thread to form a loop beneath this thread. Take the needle over the top of the main thread and down into the loop. Pull tightly.

NEEDLEWOVEN BEADING FOR DECORATIVE TRIMS

This technique involves interlacing beads using a needle and a single length of thread to achieve a solid strip of beads. The strip can be shaped by increasing or decreasing the number of beads in a row or given texture using varying sizes of beads. It is also known as diagonal bead weaving and is ideal for diagonal patterns. Designs should be charted on a piece of graph paper before starting.

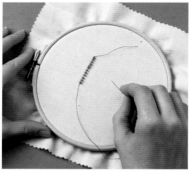

1 Lay down the first row of beads to the width of your design by threading them onto a beading needle and a long length of thread. The beads can be strung out on a cork board, secured by two pins, or stitched to a piece of fabric at either end as shown.

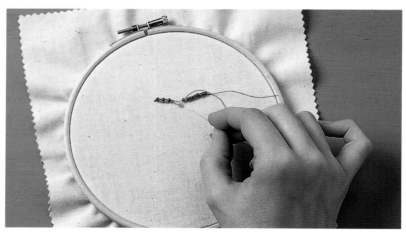

2 Pass the needle and thread back through the first bead. Thread on a new bead to sit between the first and second beads of the original row. Pass the needle through the second bead of the original row, thread on a new bead to sit between the second and third beads of this row and so on. The last new bead should sit after the last bead of the original row.

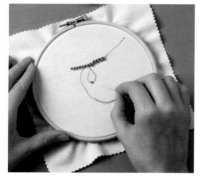

3 Continue threading the third row to sit between the pairs of beads in the second row. Once you have got the hang of beading straight strips, try increasing and decreasing to form shapes such as triangles and curves.

FRINGING

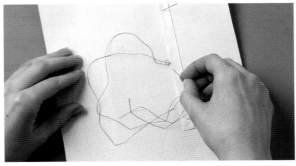

1 If your design is complicated, chart it on graph paper first. A long fringe needs to be very secure so it is advisable to attach the lengths individually. For ease, work the fringe on fabric tape pinned to a cork board, which can be attached to the object afterwards. The bead hole needs to be large enough to hold four thicknesses of bead thread. Decide on the length of fringe and for each length cut a piece of thread to four times that measurement. Double the thread and thread the two ends onto a needle. Stitch the ends through the edge of the tape and through the loop where the thread is doubled. Pull tight.

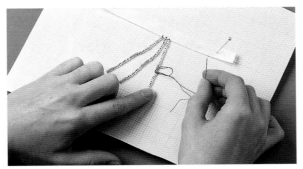

2 Thread on the beads for the fringe strand, then return the needle over the final bead and back up through half the beads. Make a fastening-off stitch about halfway up the length of the beads, then carry on passing the needle up through the beads. Make another fastening-off stitch about three beads from the top. Pull the thread gently to make sure the beads are hanging smoothly and snip off the ends of the thread.

3 For a short fringe, the beads can be attached with a continuous thread. Work out the amount of thread needed by doubling each length and adding another half extra for fastening on and off. This method can be worked directly on to the fabric but it may be easier to pin it to a cork board. Work from left to right of the design. Attach the thread to the fabric and thread on the first length of beads.

4 Return the thread around the last bead and pass the needle back up through the strand. Fasten off through the fabric and start the next strand one bead width to the right of the first. Continue, following the design until the fringe is completed.

FINISHING DROPS OR FRINGING

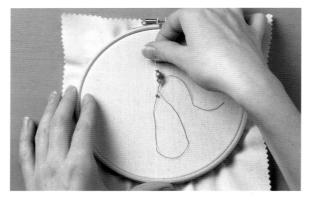

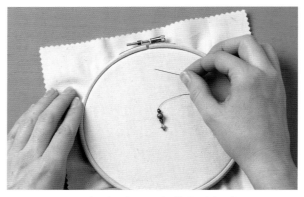

1 This is the easiest and neatest way to finish a length of fringe or a drop. Simply use a small single bead as an anchor. Thread on the beads required for the drop. Thread on the final bead. Then pass the needle around this bead and back up through the previously threaded beads.

2 Drops can be further embellished by forming an anchor from more than one bead. This time thread on the beads required for the drop, then thread on three more beads and pass the needle back up through the final bead of the drop. The three small beads form what is called a "picot" finish.

BEADED BUTTONS

1 For a random design on a fabric-covered button, make a concealed fastening-on (securing) stitch and bring the needle out through the fabric on the button. Thread on a rocaille bead and then make a small stitch and pass the needle back under the fabric. Bring it out a couple of bead-widths away and repeat until the button is covered.

2 For a flower design, make a concealed fastening-on stitch and stitch the main bead in the centre of the button. Divide the circumference of the button into equal parts and make small marks on the outside of the button with a pencil. Stitch a line of beads from the middle bead to each marked point, securing in the centre of the line as you go for extra strength. Secure the thread at the end of each line.

Couched beading

This technique is ideal for stitching beads to fabric as it results in a smoother effect and a neater continuous line than stitching down each bead individually. It is ideal for fine beadwork and can be used to work a solid motif which can be transferred and appliquéd onto another fabric.

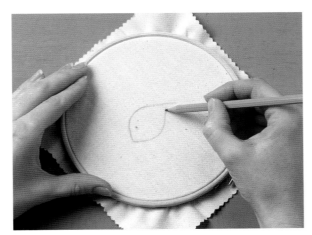

1 First draw your design in pencil as a guide for laying down the beads.

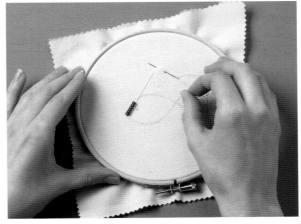

2 Lay down the beads pre-strung on a length of thread and secure in a straight line following the design, with the thread pulled taut around the needle.

3 With a separate length of thread in another needle, stitch over the original thread, working tiny stitches between each bead. After each stitch slide the bead up close so that it sits neatly next to its neighbour, and continue stitching. Follow the line of the design, moving and securing the original thread as you go.

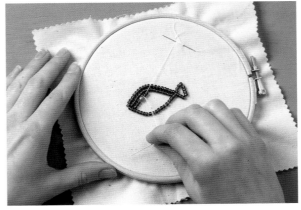

4 For a solid motif, lay the next line as close as possible to the first line and introduce other coloured beads or different shaped beads according to your design.

SEWING & FINISHING TECHNIQUES

The sewing techniques listed in this section include all the basic stitches, such as blanket stitch and gathering stitch, plus advice on different seams and hems

STITCHES

BLANKET STITCH

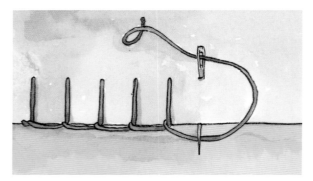

Fasten on and insert the needle 1.5cm/⅝in from the edge of the fabric. Loop the thread under the point of the needle, pull the needle through and insert it again 1cm/½in to the right of the first stitch. Continue in this way along the edge of the fabric.

STAB STITCH

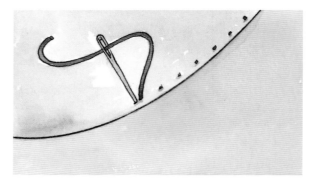

Fasten on and bring the needle up through the fabric from the underside and down again almost in the same place to catch a small amount of fabric. This stitch should be almost invisible on the right side, and is mostly used to hold layers of fabric or cord in place.

GATHERING STITCH

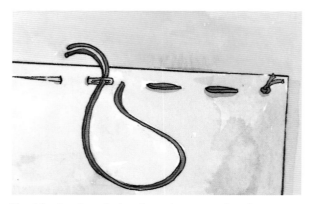

Double the thread, tie a knot in one end and sew a running stitch. Draw up the thread to form gathers.

SLIP STITCH

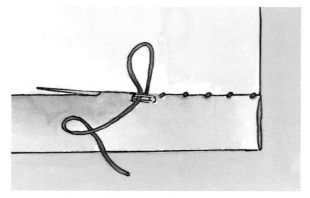

This is used to hold hems in place or to close gaps invisibly. Pick up only a few threads at a time.

SEAMS AND HEMS

PLAIN SEAM

A simple seam suitable for joining most fabrics.

1 Pin, tack (baste) and machine-stitch the two pieces of fabric, right sides together, with a 2cm/¾in seam allowance. If the fabric has a pattern, be sure it matches.

2 Remove the tacking and press the seam open. To prevent puckering at the selvedge, use sharp scissors to clip the seam allowance at 10cm/4in intervals.

FRENCH SEAM

This quick and neat seam is perfect for using with sheer or fine fabrics where a plain seam would be unsightly.

1 Pin, tack (baste) and machine-stitch the fabric, keeping the wrong sides together, with a 1cm/½in seam allowance. Trim the seam allowance a little.

2 Press the seam open then refold, this time with right sides together. Pin, tack and machine-stitch 1cm/½in from the first seam line, enclosing all raw edges.

NO-SEW SEAM

For fine and lightweight fabrics use a fusible adhesive bonding strip to make a no-sew hem.

1 Measure, fold and press the hem then place the bonding strip between the hem and the fabric. Use a hot iron to press the hem so that the adhesive melts and fuses the layers of fabric together.

CURTAIN HEADING VARIATIONS

TIES

As an alternative to a plain tab top, stitch two long tabs in pairs along the curtain top, then tie in decorative bows or knots.

EYELETS AND HOOKS

Use decorative hooks to attach a curtain to a narrow pole. Insert eyelets at approximately 15cm/6in intervals across a double hem at the top of the curtain.

DECORATIVE CLIPS

There are many decorative clips available to choose from, ideal for hanging lightweight curtains or panels without the need for stitched-on tapes. Simply clip on to the curtain and then slip on to a pole or curtain rod.

SMALL CLIPS

Small decorative clips are available for use with lightweight or sheer curtains and a pole or rod. They are ideally suited to a small window or a café-style curtain.

TENSION ROD

A tension rod is used for lightweight or café curtains in a recessed window where it is difficult to fit a track or pole. The rod is slipped through a stitched casing at the top of the curtain.

CURTAIN WIRE

Used for lightweight voiles or nets, the plastic-coated wire is trimmed to size then passed through a casing at the top of the fabric. A metal hook can then be inserted into each end ready to hook on to metal eyes screwed into the window frame.

BASIC TAB HEADING

1 Cut out a rectangle of fabric for each tab, following the template at the back of the book. Fold in half lengthways, with right sides together. Stitch together along the long edge with a 1cm/½in seam allowance.

2 For tab curtains with button fastenings or decorations, open the seam with your fingers at one end of the tab and pin together so that the seam lies at the centre of the tab. Stitch across the end with a 1cm/½in seam allowance.

3 Trim the seam allowance and snip across the corners to reduce bulk. Turn the tab through to the right side and press. Turn the tab in half widthways.

4 Pin the tabs to the right side of the curtain, matching the raw edges of the tabs to the top edge of the curtain. Lay a facing strip on top with right sides together and stitch along the top edge with a 2cm/¾in seam allowance. Fold the facing to the wrong side of the curtain and press, then fold in the seam allowance along the raw edge and stitch in place. Tuck in the raw edges at each end and slip-stitch.

CUSHIONS

BUTTONS AND BUTTONHOLES

Press a double hem twice the width of the button on both opening edges. Machine stitch the hems. Mark the button positions on the underlap and buttonholes on the overlap at even intervals, making sure that the marks match. Make each buttonhole length one-and-a-half times the width of the button. At the marked points, stitch the buttons in place: place a matchstick on the button and work a few stitches through the holes in the button; remove the matchstick and wind the thread around the shank. At the marked positions, work a close zig-zag stitch along the buttonhole. At the end mark, select a wider stitch and work a bar of six stitches. Reset the stitch and zig-zag back along the marked edge. Work another bar at this end, and back stitch to secure. Using sharp embroidery scissors or a stitch ripper, snip between the edges to make a slit.

ROULEAU LOOPS

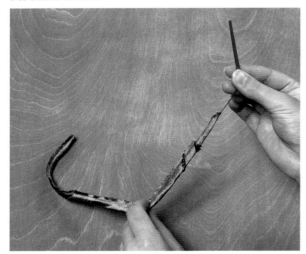

1 Cut a 3cm-/1¼in-wide bias strip of fabric. Fold it lengthways with right sides together, and machine stitch 6mm/¼in from the edge. Pass the end through a tapestry needle or on to a safety pin, and push through the tube to turn it right side out.

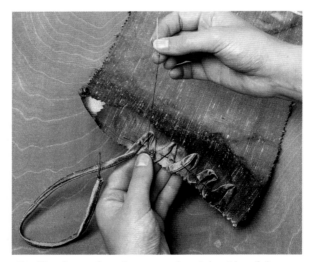

2 Pin the rouleau loops on the right side of the opening edges of the cushion cover, spacing them evenly. They should fit easily over the buttons. Tack (baste) and machine stitch the loops in place. With right sides together, pin the facing over the rouleau loops and machine stitch the seam. Turn and press the facing to the wrong side, and top stitch.

MITRING RIBBON

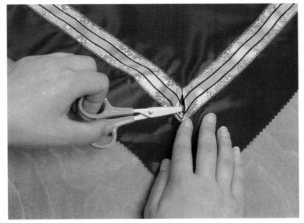

1 Starting at one corner, pin both edges of the ribbon parallel to the hem, making folds in the corner. Machine stitch all around to attach the ribbon to the fabric, and tuck the excess ribbon under at the corners to form a neat diagonal seam.

2 Next, ladder stitch the seam together. This is done by simply making horizontal stitches between the folds and running the needle through the fold.

BUTTON LOOPS

At the marked points on the folded edge, work several stitches back and forth over your finger, checking that the stitches fit comfortably over the button. Starting at one end of the stitches, work over the strands with a close blanket stitch.

FABRIC TIES

Cut pairs of ties 18 x 10cm/7 x 4in. Fold them in half lengthways and stitch one short and one long side, then clip the corners and turn right side out. Mark the positions of the ties on the right side of the opening edges of the cushion cover, making sure that they match up. Pin the ties facing inwards with raw edges matching. With right sides together, pin the facing over the ties, matching raw edges, and then machine stitch the seam.

APPLIQUÉ USING FUSIBLE BONDING WEB

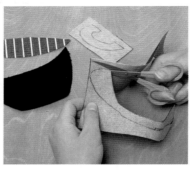

1 Enlarge the design and trace it on to the backing paper of the fusible web. Place the sticky (fusible) side face down on the wrong side of the appliqué fabric. Fuse in place with a hot iron.

2 Cut out the motif around the marked line and carefully peel away the backing paper.

3 Place the motif sticky side down on the main fabric and press with a hot iron.

MAKING BIAS BINDING

1 Cut a rectangular piece of fabric twice as long as it is wide. Hold a set square against the selvedge, or fold the fabric diagonally, to find the bias. Mark this fold with pins. From this fold draw parallel lines 4cm/1½in apart, marking as many strips as necessary using tailor's chalk and a ruler. Carefully trim away the triangular corners.

2 Pin the short edges together so that the end of one strip extends beyond the seam at the top and bottom. Stitch a 6mm/¼in seam and press open.

3 Cut along the marked lines to make one continuous length of bias binding.

MOSAIC AND GLASS TECHNIQUES

The decorative craft techniques of grouting mosaics and cutting glass are fairly easy to master.

GROUTING

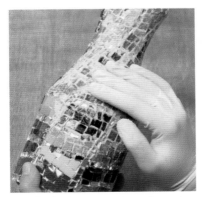

1 When grouting three dimensional objects or uneven surfaces, spread the grout with a flexible knife or spreader.

2 Rub the grout deep into the crevices between the tesserae. Wear rubber (latex) gloves when you are handling grout directly.

3 Grout large, flat mosaics with powdered tile adhesive. Spread out with a soft brush to fill the crevices. After grouting, spray the tile adhesive with water.

CUTTING GLASS

Practise this technique on scraps of glass before using a glass cutter on expensive coloured glass. It is advisable to wear protective gloves.

1 Hold the glass cutter in your palm and rest your index finger along the top. The cutter should be at a 90-degree angle to the glass.

2 Applying firm pressure, score a line across the glass in one clean movement. You can push the cutter away from you or pull it towards you. Do not score over the same line; if you make a mistake, simply try again on another part of the glass.

3 Hold the scored piece of glass in one hand. With your working hand, position pliers along the scored line and grip firmly. Angle the tip of the pliers up and pull down. The glass should break cleanly in two, along the scored line.

PAPIER-MÂCHÉ TECHNIQUES

Papier-mâché is a delightfully simple and inexpensive craft. It is possible to learn the basic techniques very quickly and produce pleasing results.

TEARING NEWSPAPER

1 If you try to tear a sheet of newspaper against the grain – from side to side – it is impossible to control.

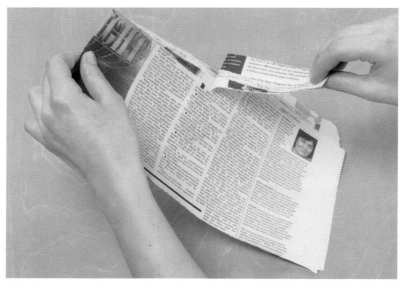

2 If newspaper is torn along the grain it is possible to produce very regular strips, as wide or narrow as you need.

PAPIER-MÂCHÉ PULP

Papier-mâché pulp is easy to make at home. Use it for moulded projects and for building up sculptures.

YOU WILL NEED
5 sheets newspaper
saucepan
spoon
blender
plastic box
5 dessertspoons (10 teaspoons)
PVA white glue
2 dessertspoons (4 teaspoons) wallpaper
paste
1 dessertspoon (2 teaspoons)
plaster of Paris
1 dessertspoon (2 teaspoons)
linseed oil

1 Tear the paper into pieces about 2.5cm/1in square and cover with water in an old saucepan. Simmer for about 30 minutes.

2 Spoon the paper and any remaining water into a blender and blend to a pulp. Pour into a suitable container. (Lidded plastic boxes are ideal, because the pulp keeps for several weeks.)

3 Add the PVA (white) glue, wallpaper paste, plaster of Paris and linseed oil. Stir vigorously, and the pulp is ready to use.

STENCILLING TECHNIQUES

Stencilling is not difficult to master, but it is worth practising on a small area to get used to handling the brush and to become accustomed to the properties of the paints you use. Some of the tips and techniques suggested below will make the task easier.

TRANSFERRING TEMPLATES

 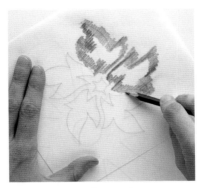 

1 To transfer a template on to a piece of stencil card or acetate, place a piece of tracing paper over the design, and draw over it with a hard pencil.

2 Turn over the tracing paper, and on the back of the design rub over the lines you have drawn with a soft pencil.

3 Turn the tracing paper back to the right side and place on top of a sheet of stencil card or acetate. Draw over the original lines with a hard pencil.

CUTTING STENCILS

1 Place the stencil on to a cutting mat or piece of thick cardboard and tape in place. Use a craft knife or scalpel for cutting.

2 It is safer to move the cutting board towards you and the knife when working round awkward shapes. Continue, moving the board as necessary.

TEMPLATES

The templates given here can be scaled up or down using a photocopier, to suit the size of your design. Always measure the object to be decorated and calculate the enlargement necessary before photocopying.

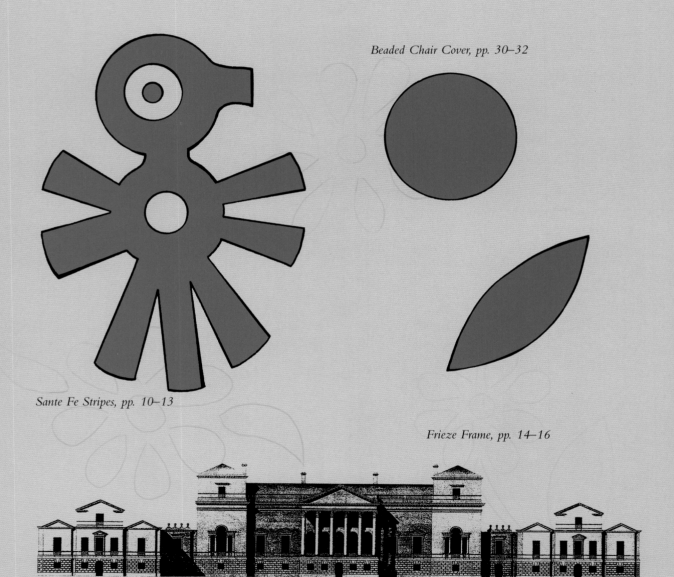

Beaded Chair Cover, pp. 30–32

Sante Fe Stripes, pp. 10–13

Frieze Frame, pp. 14–16

Seashore Bathroom Set,
pp. 174–176

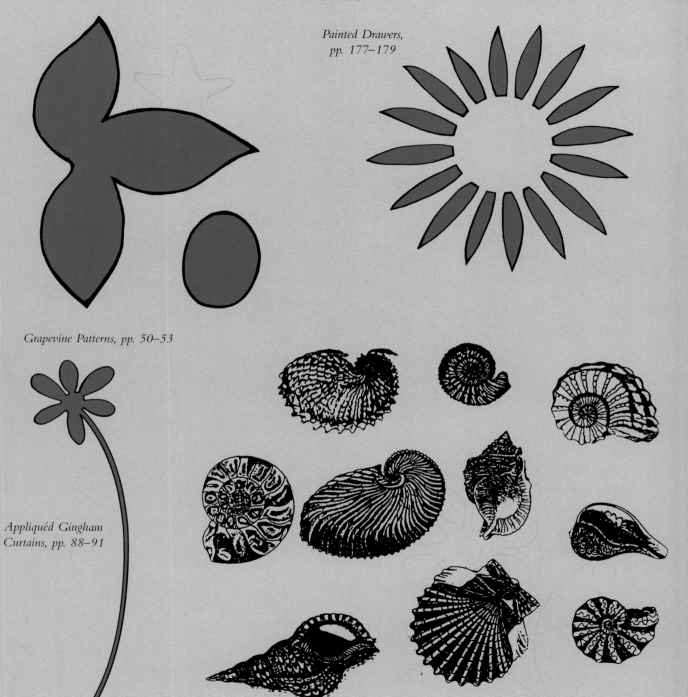

Painted Drawers,
pp. 177–179

Grapevine Patterns, pp. 50–53

Appliquéd Gingham
Curtains, pp. 88–91

Glass Nugget Window Hanging, pp.183–185

Sandcastle Frieze,
pp. 150–153

Gothic Walls, pp. 84–87

Mosaic Lamp Base,
pp. 33–37

Trinket Box,
pp. 145–147

Sunlight Catcher,
pp. 217–219

Flowers and Leaves
Lampshade,
pp. 137–141

Daisy-Covered
Console,
pp. 192–195

Leafy Window,
pp. 214–216

Valentine Mirror,
pp. 206–209

Splashback Squares
pp. 162–164

SUPPLIERS

Alec Tiranti Ltd.
70 High Street
Theale
Reading
RG7 5AR
Tel: 01734 302 775

The Bead Shop
43 Neal Street
London
WC2H 9PJ
Tel: 0181 553 3240

Beads
259 Portobello Road
London W11 1LR
Tel: 0171 792 3436

Cornelissen & Son Ltd.
105 Great Russell Street
London WC1B 3RY
Paint

Crown Paints
Crown Decorative
Products Ltd.
PO Box 37
Crown House
Hollins Road
Darwen
Lancashire
BB3 0BG

Daler-Rowney Ltd.
PO Box 10
Southern Industrial Estate
Bracknell
Berkshire
RG12 8ST

The Dover Bookshop
18 Earlham Street
London
WC2H 9LN
*Sells a wide range of
source books*

Ellis & Farrier
20 Beak Street
London
W1R 3HA
Beads and sequins

Europacrafts
Hawthorn Avenue
Hull
HU3 5JZ

Hawkin and Co.
Saint Margaret
Harleston
Norfolk
IP20 0PJ
*Decoupage by
mail order*

John Lewis Plc
Oxford Street
London
W1A 1EX
*Fabrics, furnishing fabrics,
trimmings, ribbons,
beads, curtain tapes*

Kernowcraft
Freepost
Bolingey
Perranporth
Cornwall
TR6 0DH
*Suppliers of jeweller's
round-nosed as well as
straight-nosed pliers
and fine wire-cutters.*

Lead and Light
35A Hartland Road
Camden Town
London NW1 8DB
*Suppliers of soldering and
glass-cutting equipment,
etching paste, stained glass,
copper foil and glass paints*

London Graphic Centre
16 Shelton Street
London WC2H 9JJ
Art suppliers

Mosaic Workshop
1a Princeton Street
London
EC1R 4AX
Tel: 0171 404 9249

**The Northern Beading
Company**
The Corn Exchange
Call Lane
Leeds
West Yorkshire
7BR
Tel: 0113 244 3033

**North Western Lead
Company Ltd.**
Newton Moor Industrial
Estate
Mill Street
Hyde
Cheshire
SK14 4LJ
*Suppliers of
self-adhesive lead*

Nu-Line
315 Westbourne Park Road
London
W11
*General hardware, sheet metal
supplies*

Ornamenta
3-12 Chelsea Harbour
Design Centre
Chelsea Harbour
London
SW10 0XE
*Border designs, cherubs and
print room decorations*

Paint Magic
79 Shepperton Road
Islington
London
N1 3DF

Paperchase
Tottenham Court Road
London
W1
*Paper specialists, paints and
artist's materials*

Philip and Tacey Ltd.
Tel: 01264 332171
Glass paints and contour paste.

E. Ploton Ltd.
273 Archway Road
London
N6 5AA
Tel: 0181 348 2838
Art and gilding materials

Russell & Chapple
23 Monmouth Street
London
WC2H 9DE
Canvas, calico suppliers

Stuart Stephenson Ltd.
68 Clerkenwell Road
London
EC1M 5QA

ART AND GILDING
MATERIALS

Tower Ceramics
91 Parkway
Camden Town
London
NW1 9PP
Tel: 0171 485 7192

Winsor & Newton
Whitefriars Avenue
Wealdstone
Harrow
Middlesex
HA3 5RH

Woolfin Textiles & Co.
64 Great Titchfield Street
London W1
Range of natural fabrics, calico,
hessian (burlap)

UNITED STATES

Art Essentials of
New York Ltd.
3 Cross Street
Suffern
NY 10901
Tel: 800 283 5323

Brian's Crafts Unlimited
PO Box 731046
Ormond Beach
FL 32173-046
Tel: 904 672-2726

Britex Fabrics
146 Geary Street
San Francisco
CA 94108
Fabrics, general craft
materials and equipment

Createx Colours
14 Airport Park Road
East Granby
CT 06026
Tel: 860 653 5505

Dick Blick
PO Box 1267
Galesburg
IL 61402
Tel: 309 343-6181
Wide range of general
craft items

Discount Bead
House
PO Box 186
The Plains
OH 45780
Tel: 800 793-7592

Dover
Publications Inc.
31 East 2nd Street
Mineola
NY 11501
USA

Ornamental
Resources Inc.
PO Box 3010
Idaho Springs
CO 80452
Tel: 303 567-4988

Suppliers and
Activities for
Creative Teaching
PO Box 513
Colchester
CT 06415-0513
Tel: 800 243-9232

CANADA

Abbey Arts & Crafts
4118 East Hastings Street
Vancouver BC
Tel: 299 5201

Dressew
337 W Hastings Street
Vancouver BC
Tel: 682 6196

General
Publishing
30 Lesmill Road
Donmills
Toronto
Canada

Lewiscraft
2300 Yonge Street
Toronto
Ontario
M4P 1E4
Tel: 483 2783

Pebeo Canada
Tel: 819 829 5012
Call for details of your
nearest stockist

AUSTRALIA

Camden Arts
Center Pty Ltd.
188-200 Gertrude Street
Fitzroy
Australia 3065

Hobby Co.
402 Gallery Level
197 Pitt Street
Sydney
Tel: 02 221 0666

Lincraft
Tel: 03 9875 7575
Stores in every capital city
except Darwin

Pebeo Australia
Tel: 613 9416 0611
Call for details of
your nearest stockist

Spotlight (60 stores)
Tel: freecall 1800 500021

The Stained Glass Centre
221 Hale Street
Peterie Terrace
Queensland 4000

Lincraft
Tel: 03 9875 7575
Stores in every capital city
except Darwin.
Call for details of your
nearest store.

Rosenhain,
Lipman & Peers
147 Burnley Street
Richmond
Melbourne
Victoria 3121
Paper products and scraps

INDEX

ACKNOWLEDGEMENTS

THE PUBLISHERS WOULD LIKE TO THANK THE FOLLOWING ARTISTS AND DESIGNERS WHOSE WORK APPEARS IN THIS BOOK:

MAGGIE PHILO
Projects: Dry-Brushed Chair, Misty Lilac Stripes, Hot Pink Wall, Trompe L'Oeil Tuscan Wall
Maggie Philo is a successful designer with extensive experience of creating decorative paint finishes for walls and furniture.

SACHA COHEN
Projects: Flowerpot Frieze, Grapevine Frieze, Santa Fe Stripes, Gothic Walls, Painted Drawers, Sandcastle Frieze
Sacha Cohen has a degree in Fine Art, and works as a freelance artist and set designer. She is an exciting talent in the field of paint effects, stencilling and stamping.

MARY FELLOWS
Projects: Hand-Painted Mugs, Checkerboard Dinner Plate, Seashore Bathroom Set
Mary Fellows has a degree in three-dimensional design and runs her own business, designing and painting original, and often quirky, ceramics.

DEIRDRE O'MALLEY
Projects: Kitchen Storage Jar, Painted Salt and Pepper Shakers, Etched Bathroom Mirror, Glass Nugget Window Hanging, Sunlight Catcher
Deirdre O'Malley studied three-dimensional glass and works as a sought-after glass artist.

ALISON JENKINS
Projects: Appliquéd Gingham Curtains, Ribbon Café Curtain, Stamped Calico Blind, Ribbon Flower Curtains, Leafy Window, Woven Organza Blind, Voile Striped Curtains
Alison Jenkins trained in fashion design before moving into decorative crafts. She has created ideas and written features for a number of leading magazines.

HELEN BAIRD
Projects: Daisy-Covered Console, Valentine Mirror, Splashback Squares, Spiral Vase, Trinket Box, Mosaic Lamp Base
Helen Baird is a fine arts graduate who is a well-known mosaic artist, as well as a successful freelance artist and illustrator.

JOSEPHINE WHITFIELD
Projects: Frieze Frame, Wall of Colour, Candle Shades, Door Plaque, Screen Test
Josephine Whitfield has a degree in fine art and is a leading artist in the field of painting and decoupage.

LISA BROWN
Projects: Beaded Throw, Beaded Chair Cover, Simple Bead Curtain, Beaded Wire Candlesticks, Napkin Ring and Night-Light, Beaded Cushion Trims, Beaded Wall Sconce, Fish Mosaic Splashback
Lisa Brown trained in interior design at the Chelsea School of Art in London. She was previously Style Editor of *Inspirations* magazine, and currently works as a stylist and journalist for a variety of magazines.

VICTORIA BROWN
Projects: On the Tiles, On Display
Victoria Brown trained at the Royal College of Art and now teaches art and design. Her designs are highly sought-after and appear regularly in leading lifestyle magazines.

ISABEL STANLEY
Projects: Purple Corded Lampshade, Flowers and Leaves Lampshade, Silk Trellis Cushion, Country Check Cushion, Timeless Cushion. Isabel Stanley trained in Textiles and Embroidery at Goldsmiths College in London. Her fabric work is known for its distinctive style and use of colour.

MARION ELLIOT
Projects: Pebble Wall Clock, Fish Fridge Magnets, Decoupage Waste Bin, Magazine Rack, Nautical Wall-Store, Gothic Candelabra
Marion Elliot is a well-known artist and author whose work is widely exhibited and sold in both London and New York.

THE PUBLISHERS WOULD ALSO LIKE TO THANK THE FOLLOWING PHOTOGRAPHERS:

DAVID PARMITER: for the Pebble Wall Clock, Fish Fridge Magnets, Decoupage Waste Bin, Magazine Rack, Nautical Wall-Store, Gothic Candelabra

MICHELLE GARRETT: for the Hand-Painted Mugs, Seashore Bathroom Set, Checkerboard Dinner Plate

TIM IMRIE: for the Voile Striped Curtains, Stamped Calico Blind, Ribbon Café Curtain, Ribbon Flower Curtains, Woven Organza Blind, Leafy Window, Silk Trellis Cushion, Country Check Cushion, Timeless Cushion

ADRIAN TAYLOR: for the Silk Trellis Cushion, Country Check Cushion, Timeless Cushion, Frieze Frame, Wall of Colour, Candle Shades, Door Plaque, Screen Test, Sandcastle Frieze, Painted Drawers

LIZZIE ORME: for the Kitchen Storage Jar, Painted Salt and Pepper Shakers, Etched Bathroom Mirror, Glass Nugget Wall Hanging, Leaded Door Panels, Sun Light Catcher, Sante Fe Stripes, Grapevine Patterns, Flowerpot Frieze, Gothic Walls, Purple Corded Lampshade, Flowers and Leaves Lampshade

GRAHAM RAE: On the Tiles, On Display
Lucinda Symons: Beaded Throw, Beaded Chair Cover, Simple Bead Curtain, Beaded Wire Candlesticks, Napkin Ring and Night-Light, Beaded Cushion Trims, Beaded Wall Sconce, Fish Mosaic Splashback

Debi Treloar: Mosaic Lamp Base, Spiral Vase, Stained Glass Screen, Stained Glass Candle-Holder, Trinket Box, Splashback Squares, Daisy-Covered Console, Valentine Mirror